Budget Issues Shaping a Farm Bill in 2013

Jim Monke
Specialist in Agricultural Policy

June 3, 2013

Congressional Research Service

7-5700

www.crs.gov

R42484

CRS Report for Congress ———————————————

Prepared for Members and Committees of Congress

Summary

The desire by many to redesign farm policy and reallocate the remaining farm bill baseline—in a sequestration and deficit reduction environment—is driving much of the farm bill debate this year. Several high-profile congressional and Administration proposals for deficit reduction have specifically targeted agricultural programs with mandatory funding. The political dynamics of sequestration and broader deficit reduction goals leave open difficult questions about how much and when the farm bill baseline may be reduced. In this context, Congress faces difficult choices about how much total support to provide for agriculture, and how to allocate that support among competing constituencies.

Funding to write the next farm bill is based on Congressional Budget Office (CBO) baseline projections of the cost of farm bill programs, and on varying budgetary assumptions about whether programs will continue. The CBO baseline is an estimation (projection) at a particular point in time of what federal spending on mandatory programs likely would be under current law. In May 2013, CBO projected that the current farm bill programs, if they were to continue beyond the 2008 farm bill, would cost $973 billion over the next 10 years (FY2014-FY2023). This baseline estimate already has been reduced by $6.4 billion over the same period because of the sequestration ordered on March 1, 2013.

When new bills are proposed that affect mandatory spending, their impact (or "score") is measured as a difference from the baseline. This baseline and scoring process sets the mandatory budget for considering a new farm bill.

The Senate-reported farm bill, S. 954, would reduce spending by $17.9 billion (-1.8%); and the House-reported bill, H.R. 1947, would reduce it by $33.4 billion (-3.4%). CBO noted that if sequestration was repealed and the baseline was increased by the $6.4 billion adjustment that has been taken, then the farm bill proposals would reduce spending by $24 billion (Senate) and $40 billion (House) over the next 10 years.

Moreover, some popular 2008 farm bill programs do not have a baseline to continue, and will require additional budgetary offsets if they are included in a new farm bill.

Contents

Budget Background 1

    Agriculture Appropriations Compared to Farm Bill Spending... 1

    What Is the CBO Baseline? 3

    CBO Baseline for Farm Bill Programs 4

Scores of the 2013 House and Senate Farm Bills 10

Farm Bill Budget and Baseline Issues 24

    Budget Sequestration.. 24

        FY2013 Sequestration 24

        Sequestration in the FY2014-FY2023 Baseline 27

    Nutrition Title Share of Farm Bill Baseline... 29

    Farm Bill Programs Without Baseline.. 29

    Possible Expiration and Reversion to Permanent Law.. 30

    Government-Wide Deficit Reduction Proposals 30

Figures

Figure 1. Agriculture Appropriations Relationship to Farm Bill Baseline 2

Figure 2. Ten-Year Mandatory Baseline for Farm Bill Titles 6

Figure 3. Mandatory Baseline for Farm Bill Titles, FY2014-FY2023 6

Figure 4. Ten-Year Mandatory Baseline for Non-Nutrition Agricultural Programs 9

Figure 5. Ten-Year Scores of the Senate and House 2013 Farm Bills 11

Figure 6. Score of the 2013 Senate Farm Bill S. 954, by Title and Fiscal Year............................ 13

Figure 7. Score of the 2013 House Farm Bill H.R. 1947, by Title and Fiscal Year...................... 13

Figure 8. Ten-Year Farm Bill Baseline, and Proposed Outlays in the 2013 Senate Farm
Bill S. 954 and the House Farm Bill H.R. 1947 14

Figure A-1. Original CBO Scores Farm Bill Proposals in 2012 34

Figure A-2. Updated CBO Scores Farm Bill Proposals in 2012... 34

Tables

Table 1. Baseline for Mandatory Farm Bill Programs, FY2014-FY2023 7

Table 2. 2013 Farm Bill Budget: Baseline, Scores, and Proposed Outlays, by Title 12

Table 3. Score of Mandatory Programs in S. 954 (Senate-Reported 2013 Farm Bill) 16

Table 4. Score of Mandatory Programs in H.R. 1947 (House-Reported 2013 Farm Bill)............. 20

Table 5. Sequestration in FY2013 of Agriculture and Related Agencies Appropriations
Accounts 26

Table 6. Impact of Sequestration on the May 2013 CBO Baseline for FY2014-FY2023 28

Table 7. Broad Deficit Reduction Proposals That Affect Farm Bill Programs 31

Table A-1. Baseline and Scores of 2012 Farm Bill Proposals, by Title...35

Appendixes

Appendix. Scores of the 2012 Farm Bill Proposals...33

Contacts

Author Contact Information...36

Congress periodically establishes agricultural and food policy in an omnibus farm bill.[1] The 2008 farm bill (P.L. 110-246) expired in 2012, but because Congress did not enact a new five-year farm bill in the 112th Congress, a one-year extension was enacted in the American Taxpayer Relief Act of 2012 (P.L. 112-240).[2] In 2013, the agriculture committees in the House and Senate have reported farm bills within each chamber. Floor consideration of S. 954 has occurred in the Senate, and floor action on H.R. 1947 is expected in the House.[3]

Budget issues are one of the primary factors affecting the development of a new farm bill, particularly in a Congress that is focused on deficit reduction. How much funding is available? How much might be used for deficit reduction? What are the budget issues and uncertainties?[4]

Budget Background

Agriculture Appropriations Compared to Farm Bill Spending

The total annual federal budget for agriculture-related programs is about $139 billion in FY2013, but not all of this total was farm bill spending or for farm bill programs (**Figure 1**). The total can be divided several ways using budget terms such as mandatory spending and discretionary spending, and with overlapping components based on committee jurisdiction.

Of the $139 billion appropriation, about $119 billion was for mandatory programs (entitlements both inside and outside the farm bill) and $20 billion was for discretionary programs (authorized both inside and outside the farm bill). Of the $119 billion mandatory subtotal, about $99 billion was for mandatory programs authorized in the farm bill (the farm bill "baseline," discussed later) and $20 billion was for child nutrition programs[5] authorized outside the farm bill and not in the jurisdiction of the House Agriculture Committee (**Figure 1**).

Discretionary spending is controlled by annual appropriations acts and is under the jurisdiction of the House and Senate Appropriations Committees. The farm bill may authorize appropriations for discretionary programs, but the programs are not funded until an appropriation is made. Most agency operations (salaries and expenses) are financed with discretionary funds. From a program perspective, the primary discretionary programs in agriculture appropriations include the Special Supplemental Nutrition Program for Women, Infants, and Children (WIC) and the Commodity Supplemental Food Program (CSFP); the Food and Drug Administration (FDA); agricultural research; most rural development programs; the Food for Peace and other international food aid programs; agricultural credit and administration of farm supports; meat and poultry inspection; certain conservation programs; and food marketing, plant and animal health, and regulatory programs (**Figure 1**).

---

[1] For more on the scope of a farm bill, see CRS Report RS22131, *What Is the Farm Bill?*

[2] For more on the extension of the 2008 farm bill, new expiration dates, and consequences of legislative delays, see CRS Report R42442, *Expiration and Extension of the 2008 Farm Bill.*

[3] Memo from Majority Leader Eric Cantor to House Republicans, May 3, 2013, available at http://politi.co/YsRFY0.

[4] For more on the specific policies proposed, see CRS Report R43076, *The 2013 Farm Bill: A Comparison of the Senate-Reported Bill (S. 954) and House-Reported Bill (H.R. 1947) with Current Law.*

[5] The federal "child nutrition programs" fund meals, snacks, and milk for children (and, in one program, some adults) in congregate, institutional settings. The account includes funding for the National School Lunch Program, School Breakfast Program, Child and Adult Care Food Program, Summer Food Service Program, and Special Milk Program.

Figure 1. Agriculture Appropriations Relationship to Farm Bill Baseline
(appropriated annual budget authority in billions of dollars)

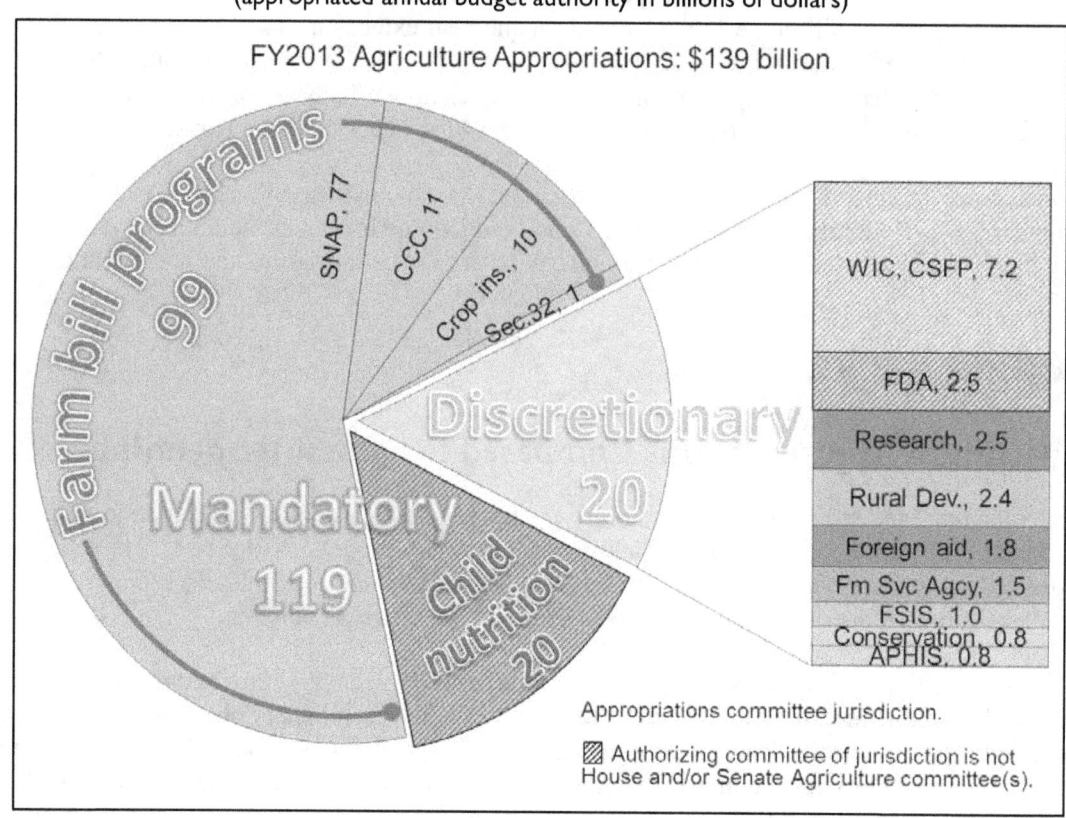

FY2013 Agriculture Appropriations: $139 billion

Farm bill programs 99

Mandatory 119

SNAP, 77

CCC, 11

Crop ins., 10

Sec.32, 1

Discretionary 20

Child nutrition 20

WIC, CSFP, 7.2

FDA, 2.5

Research, 2.5

Rural Dev., 2.4

Foreign aid, 1.8

Fm Svc Agcy, 1.5

FSIS, 1.0

Conservation, 0.8

APHIS, 0.8

Appropriations committee jurisdiction.

▨ Authorizing committee of jurisdiction is not House and/or Senate Agriculture committee(s).

Source: CRS, based on FY2013 Agriculture Appropriations Act, P.L. 113-6.

Notes: Graph is based on appropriations bill amounts and jurisdiction. Amounts reflect rescissions, but not sequestration. The amount for "other" is departmental administration, net of limitations and rescission offsets. The graph excludes the Commodity Futures Trading Commission. Authorizing committee jurisdiction generally is with House and Senate Agriculture committees, except for child nutrition and WIC (House Education and Workforce; Senate Agriculture), FDA (House Commerce; Senate Health, Education, Labor & Pensions).

SNAP = Supplemental Nutrition Assistance Program; CCC = Commodity Credit Corp.; WIC = Special Supplemental Nutrition Program for Women, Infants, and Children; CSFP = Commodity Supplemental Food Program; FDA = Food and Drug Admin.; FSA = Farm Service Agency; FSIS = Food Safety Inspection Service; APHIS = Animal and Plant Health Inspection Service.

The Agriculture appropriations bill carries—but does not pay for, nor generally determine—amounts for mandatory programs that are from authorizing legislation in the farm bill.

Mandatory spending is controlled by authorizing legislation and—for farm bill programs—is under the jurisdiction of the House and Senate Agriculture Committees. Allocating mandatory spending is one of the primary purposes of the farm bill. The farm bill "pays for" mandatory spending by creating the necessary budget authority, using resources available under budget enforcement rules. The primary mandatory spending categories in the Agriculture appropriations bill are the Supplemental Nutrition Assistance Program (SNAP, formerly called food stamps), Commodity Credit Corporation (CCC), crop insurance, some Section 32 programming, and child nutrition. The CCC is the funding mechanism for most mandatory farm bill programs, including, historically, the farm commodity programs and, in recent decades, the mandatory spending for the conservation, trade, research, horticulture, bioenergy, and rural development titles[6] of the farm bill. Section 32 is a separate mandatory fund—supported by customs receipts—created to assist non-price-supported commodities; not all farm bills have included Section 32 provisions.

Differences over what is included in the Agriculture appropriations bill compared to the farm bill primarily can be attributed to certain nutrition programs and the Food and Drug Administration. The child nutrition programs and WIC, which are in Agriculture appropriations, are not part of the farm bill because they are not in the jurisdiction of the House Agriculture Committee (the Senate Agriculture Committee does have jurisdiction). The Food and Drug Administration (FDA), part of Agriculture appropriations, is not in the jurisdiction of the House or Senate Agriculture Committees (House Commerce Committee; and Senate Health, Education, Labor & Pensions Committee). The Commodity Futures Trading Commission is in the jurisdiction of both the House and Senate Agriculture Committees, and the House Agriculture Appropriations Subcommittee (but *not* the Senate Agriculture Appropriations Subcommittee); it typically is not considered in the farm bill.

The remainder of this report focuses on mandatory spending authorized in the farm bill. For more on discretionary agriculture appropriations, see CRS Report R42596, *Agriculture and Related Agencies: FY2013 Appropriations*.

What Is the CBO Baseline?

Funding to write the next farm bill will be based on the Congressional Budget Office (CBO) baseline projection of the cost of these farm bill programs, and on varying budgetary assumptions about whether programs will continue. These amounts are shown in the CBO baseline projections for mandatory spending (direct spending) and in budget scores of proposed bills. CBO develops the baseline under the supervision of the House and Senate Budget Committees.[7] This process sets the mandatory budget for the farm bill.

The CBO baseline is an estimate (projection) at a particular point in time of what federal spending on mandatory programs likely would be under current law.[8] CBO periodically re-estimates the baseline to incorporate changes in economic conditions. When CBO makes periodic updates to the baseline, the changes do not trigger budget enforcement mechanisms but instead show how changing economic conditions affect outlays under current law. That is, increases in projected costs from last year's baseline to this year's re-estimate (e.g., because more people qualify for entitlements) do not require offsets to pay for higher costs. Likewise, reductions in projected costs from last year's baseline to this year's re-estimate (e.g., because less government intervention is needed) do not create savings that can be used to pay for other programs.

A primary purpose of the baseline is to evaluate the effect of new legislation. The baseline serves as a benchmark or starting point for changes that a bill would make. When new bills affect

---

[6] Over time, authorizing committees began providing mandatory funds to programs that generally were considered discretionary. Appropriators have argued that this reduces their oversight, and sometimes have limited outlays for the relatively newer mandatory programs using Changes in Mandatory Program Spending (CHIMPS).

[7] For more information, see CRS Report 98-560, *Baselines and Scorekeeping in the Federal Budget Process*.

[8] The most recent, detailed CBO baseline projection for agriculture is from May 2013. The baseline for the CCC (for farm commodity programs, conservation programs, and trade programs) and the Federal Crop Insurance Corporation is available at http://cbo.gov/publication/44202. The baseline for SNAP is available at http://cbo.gov/publication/44211.

mandatory spending, their impact (or "score") is measured as a difference from the baseline. Projected increases in budgetary cost above the baseline (that is, a positive score, a score greater than zero) may be subject to budget rules such as statutory or other types of PAYGO.[9] Reductions in cost below the baseline (that is, a negative score, a score less than zero) provide savings for deficit reduction or offsets that can be used to help pay for other provisions with positive scores.

From a budget perspective, programs with a continuing baseline are assumed to go on under current law, and have their own funding available for reauthorization if policymakers want them to continue. Normally, a program that receives mandatory funding in the last year of its authorization will be assumed to continue at that level of funding into the future as if there were no change in policy. This allows major farm bill provisions such as the farm commodity programs or nutrition assistance to be reauthorized periodically without assuming that funding will cease or following zero-based budgeting. However, some programs may not be assumed to continue in the budget baseline beyond the end of a farm bill because

- the program did not receive new mandatory budget authority during the last year of a farm bill, or

- the baseline during the last year of a farm bill is below a minimum $50 million scoring threshold that is needed to continue a baseline, or

- the budget committees and agriculture committees did not agree to give the program a baseline in the years beyond the end of the farm bill—either to reduce the program's 10-year cost at the time the farm bill was written, or to prevent it from having a continuing baseline.[10]

This report has a short section later about certain mandatory programs not having future baseline, but does not thoroughly explain the issue. For that discussion, see CRS Report R41433, *Expiring Farm Bill Programs Without a Budget Baseline*.

CBO Baseline for Farm Bill Programs

The May 2013 CBO baseline for mandatory farm bill programs is $973 billion for the 10-year period FY2014-FY2023 (**Figure 2**).[11] This baseline reflects a reduction of $6.4 billion over the 10-year baseline because of the effects of sequestration as ordered under the Budget Control Act of 2011.[12] Sequestration will be discussed more later in this report.

---

[9] PAYGO generally requires that direct spending and revenue legislation enacted into law not increase the deficit. It does not address deficit increases that are projected to occur under existing law, nor does it apply to discretionary spending. See CRS Report R41157, *The Statutory Pay-As-You-Go Act of 2010: Summary and Legislative History*.

[10] Section 257 of the Balanced Budget and Emergency Deficit Control Act of 1985 (P.L. 99-177, 2 U.S.C. 907), as amended, specifies that expiring mandatory spending programs are assumed to continue in the budget baseline if they have outlays of more than $50 million in the current year and were established before the Balanced Budget Act of 1997. Programs established later are not automatically assumed to continue, and are assessed program by program in consultation with the House and Senate Budget Committees. (CBO, *The Budget and Economic Outlook: Fiscal Years 2013 to 2023*, p. 22, at http://cbo.gov/sites/default/files/cbofiles/attachments/43907-BudgetOutlook.pdf).

[11] CBO, "May 2013 Baseline for the 2008 Farm Bill Programs and Provisions, by Title," unpublished, May 2013. See also "Updated Budget Projections: Fiscal Years 2013 to 2023," May 14, 2013, at http://cbo.gov/publication/44172.

[12] The effect of sequestration on the baseline is explained in the initial CBO estimates of the farm bill drafts prior to markup for the Senate farm bill (p. 2 and Table 4, at http://cbo.gov/publication/44175, May 13, 2013) and the House bill (p. 2 and Table 4, at http://cbo.gov/publication/44177, May 13, 2013).

Most of the $973 billion post-sequestration baseline is for domestic nutrition assistance programs ($764 billion, or 79%), primarily the Supplemental Nutrition Assistance Program (SNAP).[13] The rest, about $208 billion, is divided among various agriculture-related programs, primarily crop insurance ($84 billion, or 8.6%), farm commodity price and income supports ($59 billion, or 6.0%), and conservation ($62 billion, or 6.3%). Less than 1% of the baseline is for mandatory spending on international trade ($3.4 billion), horticulture programs ($1.1 billion), and the miscellaneous title ($1.4 billion for the Noninsured Assistance Program, NAP).

The baseline shows that the 2008 farm bill's programs, if they were to continue, are expected to spend about $100 billion per year through FY2016, and then decline through the rest of the baseline period to about $95 billion per year in 2023. The nutrition portion is expected to decline, while conservation and crop insurance outlays are expected to increase slightly (**Figure 3**).

Table 1 lists the baseline totals shown in **Figure 2** and **Figure 3**, and the amounts for individual programs that have baseline within each title. The table provides data for each year FY2014-FY2018, the 5-year total (FY2014-FY2018), and the 10-year total (FY2014-FY2023).

Table 1 also shows an alternative total that is slightly smaller. Some programs have baseline for expected outlays that remain from the 2008 farm bill, but are not considered to have funding available for reauthorization beyond the end of the 2008 farm bill. These include the Wetlands Reserve Program, Grasslands Reserve Program, Biomass Crop Assistance Program and other bioenergy programs, Rural Microenterprise Assistance Program, and organic and specialty crops research. Without these programs, the 10-year baseline for "continuing" farm bill programs is $949 million smaller. The alternative 10-year total is thus $972 billion, and the alternative total for the non-nutrition agricultural programs still rounds to $208 billion.

Figure 4 shows the baselines for the individual programs comprising the $208 billion 10-year subtotal of the non-nutrition programs (all of the programs except SNAP). The colors assigned to the programs are consistent with the colors of the titles in earlier figures, and show which programs in each title have the most baseline.

In the farm commodity programs, "direct payments" are the primary program with a mandatory funding baseline. Direct payments have become vulnerable politically in this high farm-income environment because they are made regardless of market price and farm income conditions.[14] The other farm commodity programs that make "counter-cyclical payments" do not have much baseline presently because high market prices for farm commodities have reduced the need for government support.

The crop insurance baseline is larger by comparison, but is considered by most farmers and policymakers to be the most important remaining component of the farm "safety net." Premium subsidies to farmers are the largest component, but reimbursements to insurance companies for delivery expenses and underwriting gains are not insignificant.

---

[13] The farm bill baseline includes SNAP but not child nutrition programs (e.g., school lunch) due to jurisdictional differences (see earlier discussion of **Figure 1**).

[14] For more background and terminology, see CRS Report R42759, *Farm Safety Net Provisions in a 2012 Farm Bill: S. 3240 and H.R. 6083.*

Figure 2. Ten-Year Mandatory Baseline for Farm Bill Titles
(10-year expected outlays FY2014-FY2023 in billions of dollars by farm bill title)

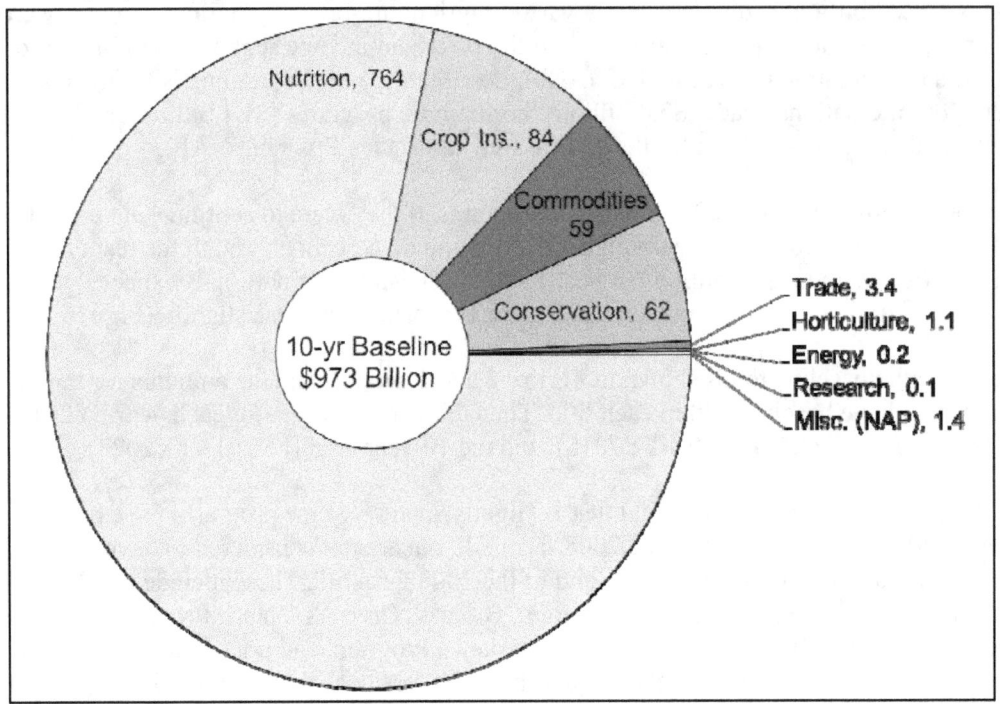

Source: CRS, using the May 2013 CBO baseline.

Figure 3. Mandatory Baseline for Farm Bill Titles, FY2014-FY2023
(annual expected outlays in billions of dollars by farm bill title)

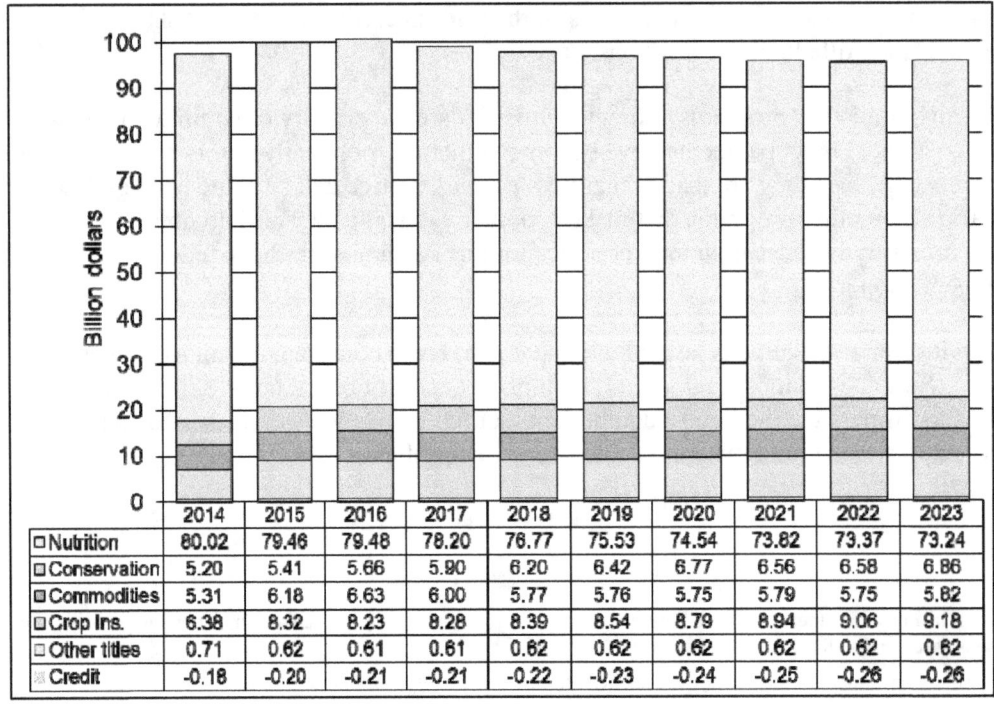

	2014	2015	2016	2017	2018	2019	2020	2021	2022	2023
Nutrition	80.02	79.46	79.48	78.20	76.77	75.53	74.54	73.82	73.37	73.24
Conservation	5.20	5.41	5.66	5.90	6.20	6.42	6.77	6.56	6.58	6.86
Commodities	5.31	6.18	6.63	6.00	5.77	5.76	5.75	5.79	5.75	5.82
Crop Ins.	6.38	8.32	8.23	8.28	8.39	8.54	8.79	8.94	9.06	9.18
Other titles	0.71	0.62	0.61	0.61	0.62	0.62	0.62	0.62	0.62	0.62
Credit	-0.18	-0.20	-0.21	-0.21	-0.22	-0.23	-0.24	-0.25	-0.26	-0.26

Source: CRS, using the May 2013 CBO baseline.

Table 1. Baseline for Mandatory Farm Bill Programs, FY2014-FY2023

(expected outlays in millions of dollars)

	Farm Bill Titles and Programs[a]	FY2014	FY2015	FY2016	FY2017	FY2018	5- and 10-year totals FY2014-FY2018	FY2014-FY2023
I	**Commodity Programs (CCC)**	**5,309**	**6,184**	**6,628**	**6,001**	**5,766**	**29,888**	**58,765**
	Direct payments	4,538	4,538	4,538	4,538	4,538	22,692	45,384
	Counter-cyclical, ACRE, Marketing loans	170	1,142	1,548	979	755	4,594	8,414
	MILC and other dairy assistance	34	34	36	32	26	161	284
	Economic assistance to cotton mills	46	48	48	48	47	237	473
	WTO Settlement with Brazil[a]	147	0	0	0	0	147	147
	Interest and operating expenses	45	90	130	144	143	552	1,259
	Other	329	331	328	259	257	1,504	2,805
II	**Conservation**	**5,203**	**5,412**	**5,660**	**5,895**	**6,203**	**28,373**	**61,567**
	Conservation Reserve Program	2,174	2,207	2,291	2,258	2,314	11,244	23,350
	Conservation Security/Stewardship Prog.	1,057	1,333	1,523	1,760	1,978	7,651	18,906
	Environmental Quality Incentives Prog.	1,233	1,365	1,474	1,524	1,565	7,161	15,240
	Farmland Protection Program	147	148	147	148	150	740	1,490
	Wildlife Habitat Incentives Program	67	73	71	75	74	360	754
	Wetlands Reserve Program[a]	370	145	21	1	0	537	537
	Agricultural Water Enhancement Prog.	60	59	57	56	56	288	568
	Chesapeake Bay Watershed Program	48	49	48	48	47	240	475
	Agricultural Management Assistance	11	13	11	11	10	56	106
	Grassland Reserve Program[a]	29	14	12	9	8	72	112
	Emergency Forestry Conserv. Reserve	5	5	5	5	1	21	26
III	**Trade (CCC)**	**344**	**344**	**344**	**344**	**344**	**1,718**	**3,435**
	Market Access Program (MAP)	200	200	200	200	200	1,000	2,000
	Export donations ocean transportation	100	100	100	100	100	500	1,000
	Foreign market development cooperator	35	35	35	35	35	173	345
	Specialty crop technical assistance	9	9	9	9	9	45	90
IV	**Nutrition (SNAP)[b]**	**80,020**	**79,457**	**79,481**	**78,204**	**76,767**	**393,930**	**764,432**
V	**Credit[c]**	**-178**	**-197**	**-205**	**-211**	**-220**	**-1,011**	**-2,240**
VI	**Rural Development**	**10**	**3**	**0**	**0**	**0**	**13**	**13**
	Rural Microenterprise Assistance Prog.[a]	10	3	0	0	0	13	13
VII	**Research and Related Matters**	**93**	**18**	**0**	**0**	**0**	**111**	**111**
	Organic; Specialty Crop; Beg. Farmers[a]	93	18	0	0	0	111	111
VIII	**Forestry**	**2**	**1**	**0**	**0**	**0**	**3**	**3**
	Healthy Forest Reserve Program[a]	2	1	0	0	0	3	3

	Farm Bill Titles and Programs[a]	FY2014	FY2015	FY2016	FY2017	FY2018	5- and 10-year totals	
							FY2014-FY2018	FY2014-FY2023
IX	**Energy**	**8**	**5**	**21**	**23**	**27**	**84**	**243**
	Feedstock Flexibility Program	0	0	19	23	27	69	228
	Other (expiring programs, incl. BCAP)[a]	8	5	2	0	0	15	15
X	**Horticulture and Organic Agriculture**	**116**	**105**	**105**	**105**	**105**	**536**	**1,061**
	Specialty Crop Block Grants	55	55	55	55	55	275	550
	Plant Pest & Disease Management	50	50	50	50	50	250	500
	Farmers Markets; Clean Plant Network[a]	11	0	0	0	0	11	11
XI	**Crop Insurance**	**6,380**	**8,325**	**8,227**	**8,276**	**8,386**	**39,592**	**84,105**
	Premium Subsidy	4,477	5,830	5,770	5,819	5,919	27,815	59,545
	Delivery Expenses	1,047	1,380	1,354	1,343	1,335	6,459	13,175
	Underwriting Gains	856	1,115	1,103	1,113	1,132	5,318	11,384
XII	**Miscellaneous**	**141**	**141**	**141**	**141**	**141**	**705**	**1,410**
	Noninsured Crop Assistance Program	141	141	141	141	141	705	1,410
	Total—Farm Bill Baseline	**97,447**	**99,797**	**100,402**	**98,776**	**97,519**	**493,941**	**972,905**
	Nutrition	80,020	79,457	79,481	78,204	76,767	393,930	764,432
	Non-nutrition	17,427	20,340	20,920	20,573	20,752	100,011	208,473
	Alternate total							
	Minus baseline of programs not continuing[a]	*-670*	*-186*	*-35*	*-10*	*-8*	*-909*	*-949*
	Remainder for continuing programs	*96,777*	*99,611*	*100,367*	*98,766*	*97,511*	*493,032*	*971,956*
	Remainder for non-nutrition programs	*16,757*	*20,154*	*20,885*	*20,563*	*20,744*	*99,102*	*207,524*

Source: CRS, using the May 2013 CBO baseline.

a. Some programs have outlays listed during the baseline period but are not considered to have funding (budget authority) to continue beyond the end of the 2008 farm bill. Other programs and titles in the 2008 farm bill are not listed because they do not have future budget baseline, even though they received mandatory funding in FY2008-FY2012. These are discussed in CRS Report R41433, *Expiring Farm Bill Programs Without a Budget Baseline*.

b. The nutrition title of the farm bill includes only the Supplemental Nutrition Assistance Program (SNAP) and related programs, given joint jurisdiction between the House and Senate Agriculture committees. Child nutrition programs, while in the jurisdiction of the Senate Agriculture Committee, are not in the jurisdiction of the House Agriculture Committee. Child nutrition programs, if included, would add $246 billion of baseline over 10 years (http://cbo.gov/publication/44186).

c. The Credit title has negative outlays that reflect receipts into the Farm Credit System Insurance Fund.

Figure 4. Ten-Year Mandatory Baseline for Non-Nutrition Agricultural Programs

(expected outlays over FY2013-FY2022 in billions of dollars for programs in a subset of farm bill titles)

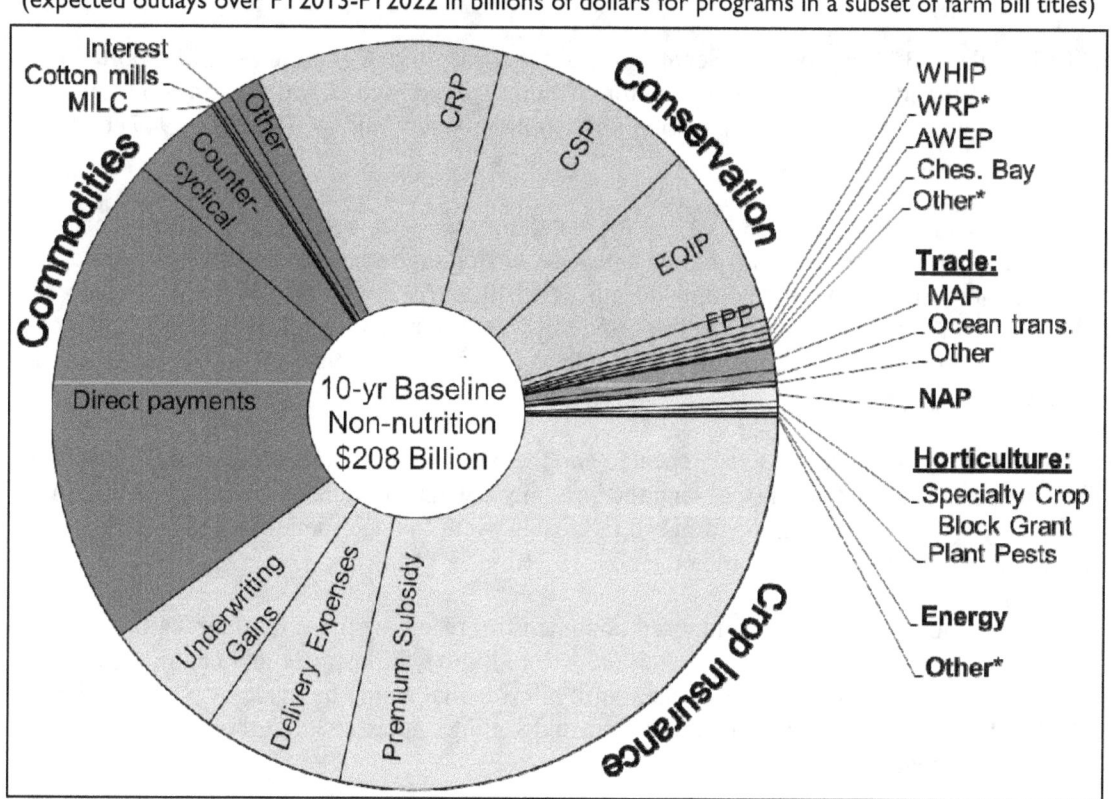

Source: CRS, using the May 2013 CBO baseline.

Notes: MILC = Milk Income Loss Contract Program; CRP=Conservation Reserve Program; CSP = Conservation Security/Stewardship Program; EQIP = Environmental Quality Incentives Program; FPP = Farmland Protection Program; WHIP = Wildlife Habitat Incentive Program; WRP = Wetlands Reserve Program; AWEP = Agricultural Water Enhancement Program; MAP=Market Access Program; NAP = Noninsured Crop Assistance Program. Includes baseline for expiring programs (*) that do not have baseline to continue, as noted in **Table 1**.

Total estimated costs of the conservation programs are now about as large as estimated farm commodity spending. The largest three conservation programs have 93% of total conservation baseline (the Conservation Reserve Program, the Conservation Security Program, and the Environmental Quality Incentives Program).

Two other farm bill titles have more than $1 billion of 10-year baseline. The Trade title has $3.4 billion, with most of it in the Market Access Program (MAP). The Horticulture and Organic Agriculture title has $1.1 billion of 10-year baseline, with half in specialty crop block grants, and half for pest and disease prevention. The Miscellaneous title has $1.4 billion of continuing 10-year baseline for the Noninsured Assistance Program (NAP). The Energy title has $0.2 billion of 10-year baseline for continuing programs, specifically the Feedstock Flexibility program to convert sugar to ethanol. The Forestry, Research, and Rural Development titles are combined under "Other" in the figure and do not have programs with baseline for reauthorization. The Credit title is not shown because it has a negative baseline, reflecting receipts into a Farm Credit System insurance fund.

Scores of the 2013 House and Senate Farm Bills

In 2013, in the 113th Congress, the Senate and House Agriculture Committees have reported farm bills out of committee. The Senate Agriculture Committee reported its bill (S. 954) on May 14, 2013, by a vote of 15-5. The House Agriculture Committee reported its bill (H.R. 1947) on May 15, 2013, by a vote of 36-10.[15]

Compared to the CBO May 2013 baseline for mandatory farm bill spending of $973 billion (discussed in the previous section, and on a post-sequestration basis), the Senate Agriculture Committee-reported farm bill would reduce spending by $17.9 billion (-1.8%) over 10 years,[16] and the House Agriculture Committee-reported bill would reduce it by $33.4 billion (-3.4%) over 10 years.[17] Even though the farm bills would expire after 5 years, budget rules require bills to be evaluated over 10 years.

CBO noted that if sequestration was repealed and the baseline was increased by the $6.4 billion adjustment that has been taken (restoring the baseline to what would have been a $979 billion baseline, hypothetically), then the farm bill proposals would reduce spending by $24 billion (Senate) and $40 billion (House) over the next 10 years.[18]

The net reduction in each bill is composed of some titles receiving more funding than in the past, while other titles provide offsets for deficit reduction. **Figure 5** illustrates the magnitude of the budgetary reductions and additions to each farm bill title that would be made by S. 954 and H.R. 1947. **Table 2** contains the data in tabular form and includes an estimate of the proposed outlays under the draft legislation.

- Under the Senate bill, seven titles would receive a combined $7.3 billion increase relative to their baselines, and four titles would offer a combined budgetary reduction of $25.2 billion. The net reduction is therefore $17.9 billion over the 10-year period FY2014-FY2023.

- Under the House bill, seven titles would receive a combined $10.6 billion increase relative to their baselines, and three titles would offer a combined budgetary reduction of $44.0 billion. The net reduction is therefore $33.4 billion over the 10-year period FY2014-FY2023.

One of the most noticeable budget differences between House and Senate bills is the reduction proposed for the nutrition title, with the Senate bill reducing it by $3.9 billion over 10 years and

---

[15] In 2012, in the 112th Congress, both the Senate and House Agriculture Committees marked up drafts for a 2012 farm bill. The Senate passed its version (S. 3240) on June 21, 2012, by a vote of 64-35. The House Committee on Agriculture reported its version (H.R. 6083) on July 11, 2012, by a vote of 35-11. House floor action, however, never occurred, and a one-year extension was enacted (P.L. 112-240). The budgetary effects of the 2012 proposals, including a re-estimate of the effects in 2013, are discussed in the **Appendix**.

[16] CBO cost estimate of S. 954 as reported by the Senate Agriculture committee (http://cbo.gov/publication/44248, May 17, 2013).

[17] CBO cost estimate of H.R. 1947 as reported by the House Agriculture committee (http://cbo.gov/publication/44271, May 23, 2013).

[18] The effect of sequestration on the baseline and scores is explained in the initial CBO estimates of the farm bill drafts prior to markup for the Senate farm bill (p. 2 and Table 4, at http://cbo.gov/publication/44175, May 13, 2013) and the House bill (p. 2 and Table 4, at http://cbo.gov/publication/44177, May 13, 2013).

---

the House bill reducing it by $20.5 billion over 10 years. This $16.6 billion difference between the bills has emerged as one of the most important political issues for the bill in 2013—especially in the House—with some calling for less reduction and others for more.

For crop insurance and the farm commodity programs, the House bill makes a bigger net reduction to the farm commodity programs than the Senate bill—reducing the Title I baseline by $1.2 billion more than the Senate bill over 10 years. Both bills recognize about $46 billion of savings by repealing direct payments, counter-cyclical payments, and the average crop revenue election, but both create new counter cyclical-type payment programs that cost at least $23 billion in each bill and reauthorize certain disaster assistance programs. For crop insurance, the House bill increases it more than the Senate bill, providing $3.9 billion more to Title XI than the Senate bill. The net result for the combination of crop insurance and farm commodities is that the House bill spends $2.7 billion more than the Senate bill (that is, the combined net savings from Title I and Title XI in the Senate bill is $12.4 billion, compared with net savings in the House bill of $9.7 billion).

Conservation changes are similar in many regards between the bills, though the House bill saves $1.3 billion more than the Senate bill in Title II. Energy (Title IX) receives more funding in the Senate bill but none in the House bill.

Figure 5. Ten-Year Scores of the Senate and House 2013 Farm Bills

(change in outlays over FY2014-FY2023 in billions of dollars by farm bill title, relative to baseline)

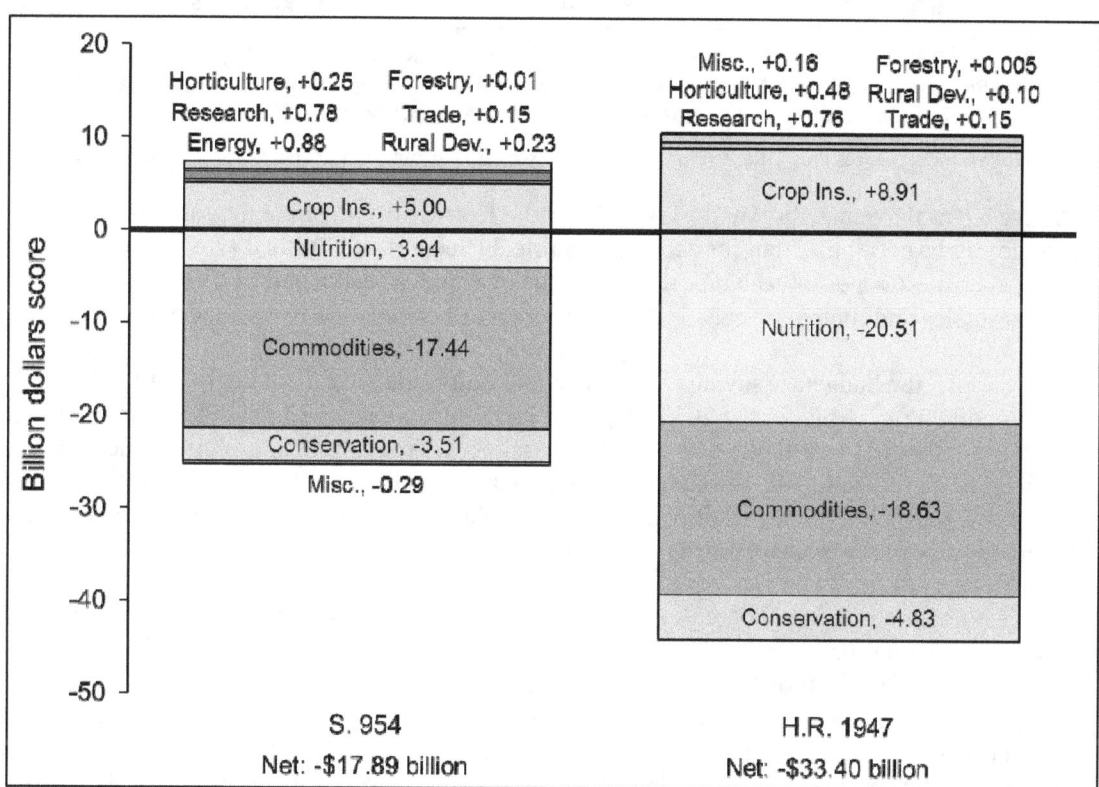

Source: CRS, using CBO cost estimates of S. 954 as reported by the Senate Agriculture committee (http://cbo.gov/publication/44248, May 17, 2013), and H.R. 1947 as reported by the House Agriculture committee (http://cbo.gov/publication/44271, May 23, 2013),

Notes: Incorporates into Title X (Horticulture) the scores of promotion orders that are classified as revenue.

Table 2. 2013 Farm Bill Budget: Baseline, Scores, and Proposed Outlays, by Title

(outlays in millions of dollars, 10-year total FY2014-FY2023)

	2013 Farm Bill Titles	CBO baseline	CBO Score of Bill (change to baseline)		Outlays Proposed (Baseline + Score)	
			S. 954	H.R. 1947	S. 954	H.R. 1947
I	Commodities	58,765	-17,442	-18,626	41,323	40,139
II	Conservation	61,567	-3,511	-4,827	58,056	56,740
III	Trade	3,435	+150	+150	3,585	3,585
IV	Nutrition	764,432	-3,944	-20,509	760,488	743,923
V	Credit	-2,240	+0	+0	-2,240	-2,240
VI	Rural Dev.	13	+228	+96	241	109
VII	Research	111	+781	+760	892	871
VIII	Forestry	3	+10	+5	13	8
IX	Energy	243	+880	+0	1,123	243
X	Horticulture	1,061	+250	+479	1,311	1,540
XI	Crop Ins.	84,105	+4,999	+8,914	89,104	93,019
XII	Misc.	1,410	-294	+161	1,116	1,571
	Total	**972,905**	**-17,894**	**-33,397**	**955,012**	**939,508**

Source: CRS, using the CBO baseline (May 2013, at http://cbo.gov/publication/44177) and CBO cost estimates of S. 954 as reported by the Senate Agriculture Committee (http://cbo.gov/publication/44248, May 17, 2013), and H.R. 1947 as reported by the House Agriculture Committee (http://cbo.gov/publication/44271, May 23, 2013).

Notes: Incorporates into Title X (Horticulture) the scores of promotion orders that are classified as revenue.

Figure 6 (for the Senate bill) and **Figure 7** (for the House bill) illustrate the same budgetary changes by farm bill title, but for each year. **Table 3** (Senate) and **Table 4** (House) present the detailed cost estimates of each bill, relative to the baseline, as estimated by CBO. These year-by-by year tables and figures reveal additional differences between the House and Senate bills.

For example, the budgetary savings from the commodity title would not begin until FY2015, because direct payments for the 2013 crop year under the extension of the 2008 farm bill are paid in FY2014, the first year of the new farm bill baseline. Changes to both crop insurance and conservation grow gradually through the budget window, with more of the effect in the second five years. Conservation has additional spending in the first three years, relative to the baseline, before savings occur in years four through ten.

Figure 8 illustrates the total outlays expected for farm bill programs under the current law baseline, and after incorporating the changes proposed in S. 954 and H.R. 1947. The first stacked bar is the same $973 billion baseline distribution from **Figure 2**. The Senate bill's $17.9 billion reduction over 10 years would reduce expected outlays to $955 billion over the FY2014-FY2023 period (the second bar). The House bill's $33.4 billion reduction would reduce outlays to $940 billion (the third bar). The net spending by the two farm bill proposals over the next 10 years would be the same whether one quotes pre- or post- sequestration estimates, since restoring the sequestration reduction to the baseline increases the savings in the bills by the same amount, as explained by CBO.

Figure 6. Score of the 2013 Senate Farm Bill S. 954, by Title and Fiscal Year

(change in outlays in billions of dollars by farm bill title, relative to baseline)

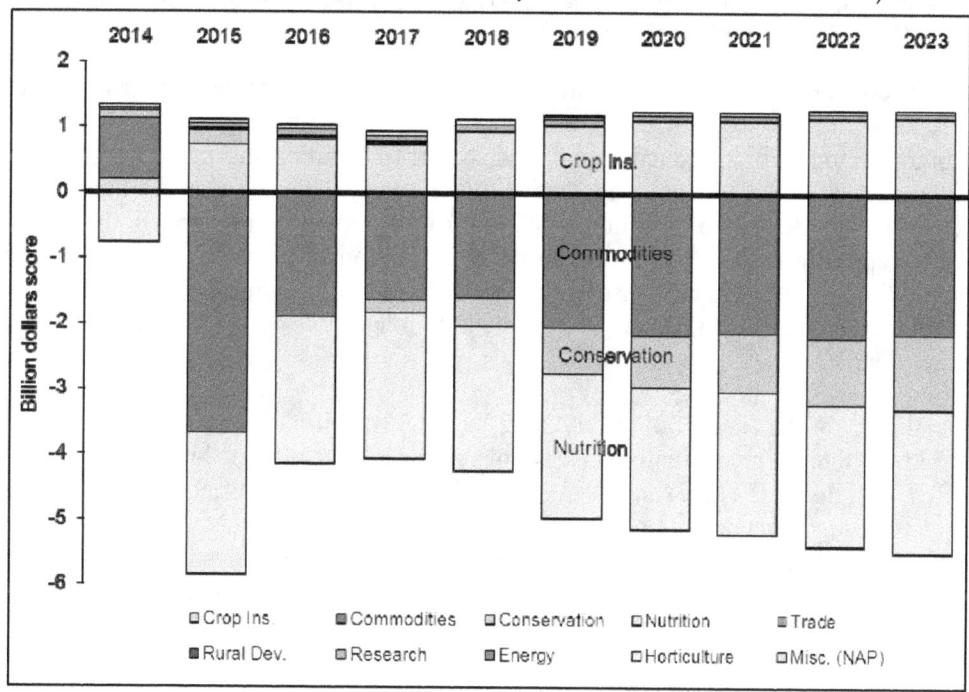

Source: CRS, using CBO cost estimates of Senate-reported S. 954, May 17, 2013.

Figure 7. Score of the 2013 House Farm Bill H.R. 1947, by Title and Fiscal Year

(change in outlays in billions of dollars by farm bill title, relative to baseline)

Source: CRS, using CBO cost estimates of House-reported H.R. 1947, May 23, 2013.

Figure 8. Ten-Year Farm Bill Baseline, and Proposed Outlays in the 2013 Senate Farm Bill S. 954 and the House Farm Bill H.R. 1947

(outlays over FY2014-FY2023 in billions of dollars by farm bill title)

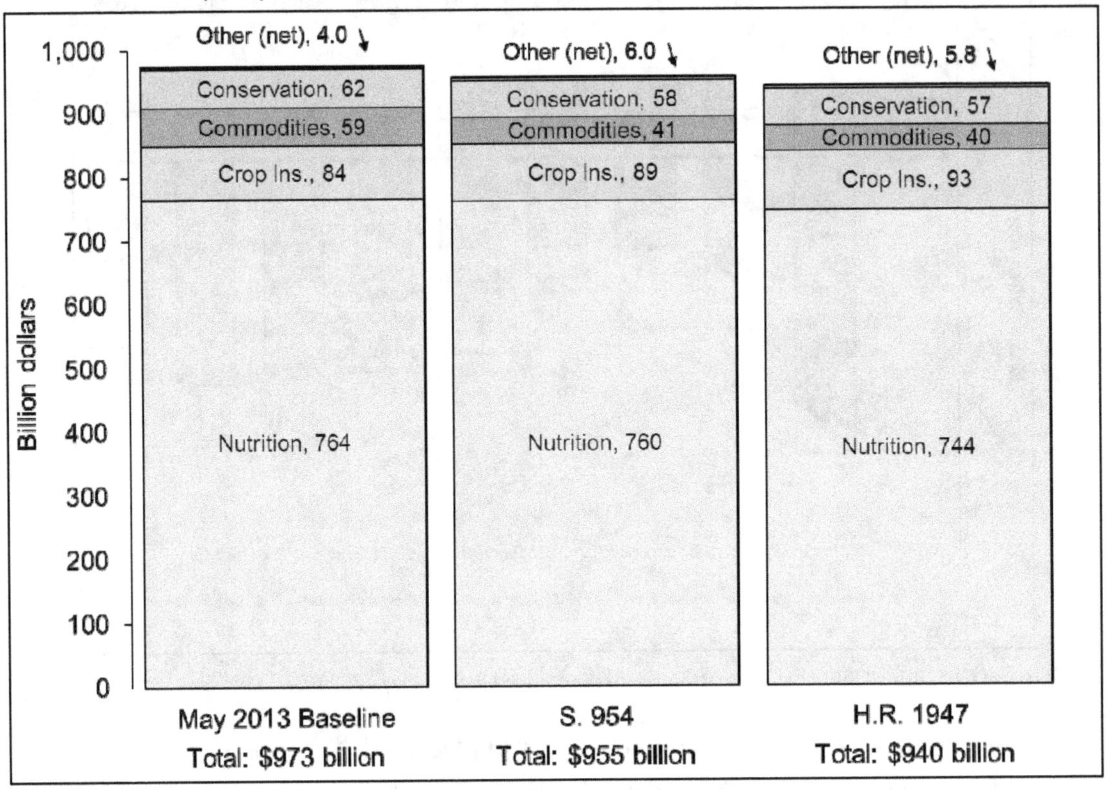

Other (net), 4.0	Other (net), 6.0	Other (net), 5.8
Conservation, 62	Conservation, 58	Conservation, 57
Commodities, 59	Commodities, 41	Commodities, 40
Crop Ins., 84	Crop Ins., 89	Crop Ins., 93
Nutrition, 764	Nutrition, 760	Nutrition, 744
May 2013 Baseline	**S. 954**	**H.R. 1947**
Total: $973 billion	Total: $955 billion	Total: $940 billion

(Y-axis: Billion dollars, 0 to 1,000)

Source: CRS, using the CBO May 2013 baseline, and CBO cost estimates of Senate-reported S. 954 (May 17, 2013), and House-reported H.R. 1947 (May 23, 2013).

The original score of the Senate bill in June 2012 with $23.1 billion of savings was consistent with the total savings proposed by the House and Senate Agriculture committees for the Joint Select Committee on Deficit Reduction (a.k.a. the Super Committee, discussed later) in the fall of 2011. The reduction in S. 954 from the nutrition title is nearly the same as in the Super Committee proposal. And the $13 billion reduction from commodity programs in the Super Committee proposal was roughly the same as the $12.4 billion of net savings in S. 954 from the farm commodity program and crop insurance. The $24 billion in savings in S. 954, if sequestration reductions were restored, is consistent with the score of the 2012 bill and the Super Committee proposal.

The original score of the House bill in July 2012, with $35.1 billion of savings, was consistent with the $33.2 billion of reconciliation instructions in the FY2013 House budget resolution (H.Con.Res. 112, discussed later) and the $35.8 billion of savings identified by the Agriculture Committee for budget reconciliation. A primary difference, though, is that all of the reconciliation savings were from nutrition programs, while more than half of the savings in H.R. 1947 are from nutrition programs. The House bill in 2013 is proposing to make greater reductions than last year's proposals.

Also, **Table 3** and **Table 4** indicate which programs in a new farm bill might become concerns over "programs without baseline" in the future.[19] The scores for the FY2019-FY2023 period reveal which programs would receive baseline beyond the expected five-year life of a new farm bill and which would receive baseline only for the five-year window of the bill (see footnote 10, and a discussion in the Issues section later). For example, the specialty crops research program would receive a 10-year baseline in the Senate bill, but three other research programs would receive baseline only through FY2018. This also is an issue for all of the programs in the Senate bill's energy and rural development titles, the farmers market promotion program, outreach for socially disadvantaged farmers, among other programs. The House bill has similar issues, such as for organic research and extension, the beginning farmers development program, the farmers market promotion program, and value-added marketing grants, among other programs.

Finally, separate from the mandatory spending figures above, the CBO cost estimates include a projection of discretionary appropriations that would be needed to carry out the authorized farm bill programs. For S. 954 and H.R. 1947, CBO estimated that $30.1 billion and $27.4 billion, respectively, of discretionary appropriations would be needed over the five-year period FY2014-FY2018. However, not all of these amounts represented new programs or spending, since much of the totals were for reauthorizing programs that are already appropriated in the annual Agriculture appropriations bill. Moreover, these amounts would be subject to annual decisions by the budget committees and the appropriations committees.

---

[19] For more background, see a discussion later in the Issues section and CRS Report R41433, *Expiring Farm Bill Programs Without a Budget Baseline.*

Table 3. Score of Mandatory Programs in S. 954 (Senate-Reported 2013 Farm Bill)

(change in annual outlays in millions of dollars, relative to baseline)

	Fiscal year										5- and 10 year total	
	2014	2015	2016	2017	2018	2019	2020	2021	2022	2023	2014-18	2014-23
Title I - Commodity Programs												
Repeal Direct Payments	0	-4,538	-4,538	-4,538	-4,538	-4,538	-4,538	-4,538	-4,538	-4,538	-18,152	-40,842
Repeal Countercyclical Payments	0	0	-117	-182	-190	-215	-217	-207	-197	-194	-489	-1,519
Repeal Average Crop Revenue Election Payments	0	0	-1,336	-696	-462	-424	-413	-454	-429	-505	-2,494	-4,719
Popcorn as a Covered Commodity	0	9	11	12	10	10	10	10	11	11	42	94
Adverse Market Payments	0	0	399	433	419	369	360	362	357	361	1,251	3,060
Agricultural Risk Coverage	0	0	3,632	3,875	3,483	2,704	2,385	2,617	2,408	2,646	10,990	23,749
Nonrecourse Marketing Assistance Loans	0	6	7	5	5	4	4	6	6	5	23	48
Sugar Program	0	0	0	0	0	0	0	0	0	0	0	0
Dairy Program	-34	-20	-9	34	57	14	94	58	59	49	28	302
Supplemental Agriculture Disaster Assistance	424	364	201	197	197	197	199	200	201	202	1,383	2,382
Administration	82	6	-11	-11	-10	-10	-10	-11	-11	-11	56	3
Subtotal, Title I	**472**	**-4,173**	**-1,761**	**-871**	**-1,029**	**-1,889**	**-2,126**	**-1,957**	**-2,133**	**-1,974**	**-7,362**	**-17,442**
Title II - Conservation												
Conservation Reserve Program	25	37	-31	-217	-324	-446	-364	-434	-458	-519	-510	-2,731
Conservation Stewardship Program	-7	-50	-87	-130	-173	-221	-265	-308	-351	-394	-447	-1,986
Environmental Quality Incentives Program	-39	-31	-8	-4	1	4	7	27	28	28	-81	13
Agricultural Conservation Easement Program	57	191	289	319	214	112	76	66	57	57	1,070	1,438
Regional Conservation Partnership Program	3	5	6	5	7	7	7	7	7	7	26	61
Other Conservation Programs	158	8	8	8	8	0	0	0	0	0	190	190
Funding	10	10	10	10	10	10	10	10	10	10	50	100

	\multicolumn{10}{c	}{Fiscal year}	5- and 10 year total	
	2014	2015	2016	2017	2018	2019	2020	2021	2022	2023	2014-18	2014-23
Repeal of Wildlife Habitat Incentives Program	-17	-35	-44	-53	-61	-70	-79	-79	-79	-79	-210	-596
Subtotal, Title II	**190**	**135**	**143**	**-62**	**-318**	**-604**	**-608**	**-711**	**-786**	**-890**	**88**	**-3,511**
Title III - Trade	**15**	**15**	**15**	**15**	**15**	**15**	**15**	**15**	**15**	**15**	**75**	**150**
Title IV - Nutrition												
Food Distribution on Indian Reservations	6	6	6	5	6	6	6	6	6	7	29	60
Standard Utility Allowances	-90	-400	-440	-450	-450	-450	-450	-450	-460	-470	-1,830	-4,110
Retail Food Stores	-7	-8	-8	-8	-8	-8	-8	-8	-8	-8	-39	-79
Funding of Employment and Training Programs	5	5	5	5	1	1	1	1	1	1	21	26
Emergency Food Assistance	22	18	10	4	0	0	0	0	0	0	54	54
Retailer Trafficking	3	2	0	0	0	0	0	0	0	0	5	5
Hunger-Free Communities	6	14	19	20	22	14	5	0	0	0	81	100
Subtotal, Title IV	**-55**	**-363**	**-408**	**-424**	**-429**	**-437**	**-446**	**-451**	**-461**	**-470**	**-1,679**	**-3,944**
Title V - Credit	**0**	**0**	**0**	**0**	**0**	**0**	**0**	**0**	**0**	**0**	**0**	**0**
Title VI - Rural Development												
Value-Added Marketing Grants	0	5	8	12	13	13	8	4	0	0	38	63
Rural Microenterprise Program	1	2	3	3	3	2	1	0	0	0	12	15
Rural Water and Waste Disposal	8	30	42	30	21	13	6	0	0	0	131	150
Subtotal, Title VI	**9**	**37**	**53**	**45**	**37**	**28**	**15**	**4**	**0**	**0**	**181**	**228**
Title VII - Research, Extension, and Related Matters												
Organic Agriculture Research and Extension	8	13	16	16	16	8	3	0	0	0	69	80
Specialty Crop Research	13	23	29	48	50	53	50	50	50	50	163	416
Beginning Farmer and Rancher Development	4	9	14	17	17	13	8	3	0	0	61	85
Foundation for Food and Agriculture Research	20	40	40	60	40	0	0	0	0	0	200	200

	Fiscal year										5- and 10 year total	
	2014	2015	2016	2017	2018	2019	2020	2021	2022	2023	2014-18	2014-23
Subtotal, Title VII	45	84	99	141	123	74	61	53	50	50	492	781
Title VIII - Forestry	1	1	1	1	1	1	1	1	1	1	5	10
Title IX - Energy												
Biorefinery Assistance	0	30	47	55	44	25	12	3	0	0	176	216
Rural Energy for America Program	14	42	60	68	68	56	26	6	0	0	252	340
Biomass Research and Development	1	5	16	25	26	25	21	10	1	0	73	130
Biomass Crop Assistance Program	4	12	20	27	31	29	23	16	8	4	94	174
Other Energy Programs	4	4	4	4	4	0	0	0	0	0	20	20
Subtotal, Title IX	23	93	147	179	173	135	82	35	9	4	615	880
Title X - Horticulture												
Farmers Market and Local Food Promotion	20	20	20	20	20	0	0	0	0	0	100	100
Coordinated Plant Management Program	3	6	8	9	11	13	14	15	15	15	36	108
Specialty Crop Block Grants	8	14	15	15	15	15	15	15	15	15	66	141
Other Horticulture Programs	2	0	-2	-2	-3	-5	-7	-7	-10	-10	-5	-44
Subtotal, Title X outlays	32	39	41	42	43	23	21	22	20	20	197	304
Revenue: Organic Product Promotion Orders	0	-2	-4	-4	-5	-5	-7	-7	-10	-10	-15	-54
Subtotal, Title X	32	37	37	38	38	18	14	15	10	10	182	250
Title XI - Crop Insurance												
Supplemental Coverage Option	14	141	187	208	256	266	287	286	300	303	806	2,247
Catastrophic Crop Insurance Rerating	-4	-38	-50	-52	-52	-53	-54	-55	-55	-56	-196	-469
Enterprise Units Irriganted/Nonirrigated Crops	5	47	62	63	64	66	68	69	71	72	241	586
Adjustment in Average Producer History Yields	1	9	21	33	45	56	59	60	61	62	108	406
Stacked Income Protection for Cotton	36	350	378	308	386	409	439	451	468	466	1,459	3,693

	Fiscal year										5- and 10 year total	
	2014	2015	2016	2017	2018	2019	2020	2021	2022	2023	2014-18	2014-23
Peanut Revenue Crop Insurance	3	26	30	30	30	30	30	30	30	30	119	269
Implementation	2	21	16	15	15	14	2	0	0	0	69	85
Beginning Farmer Provisions	2	20	26	28	31	34	35	36	36	36	106	283
Crop Production on Native Sod	0	-5	-12	-18	-23	-24	-24	-24	-24	-24	-58	-178
Conservation Compliance for Crop Insurance	0	0	0	-2	-3	-5	-8	-8	-8	-8	-5	-42
Participation Effects of Commodity Programs	0	-28	-277	-331	-301	-241	-213	-224	-212	-210	-938	-2,038
Other	2	21	28	29	30	28	8	5	3	2	110	156
Subtotal, Title XI	**61**	**563**	**409**	**311**	**477**	**579**	**629**	**626**	**669**	**673**	**1,821**	**4,999**
Title XII - Miscellaneous												
Outreach for Socially Disadvantaged Farmers	5	8	10	10	10	5	2	0	0	0	43	50
Sheep Production and Marketing Grant Program	1	1	0	0	0	0	0	0	0	0	2	2
Noninsured Crop Disaster Assistance Program	6	48	-36	-52	-52	-52	-52	-52	-52	-52	-86	-346
Subtotal, Title XII	**12**	**57**	**-26**	**-42**	**-42**	**-47**	**-50**	**-52**	**-52**	**-52**	**-41**	**-294**
Net Impact on the Deficit	**806**	**-3,514**	**-1,292**	**-669**	**-954**	**-2,127**	**-2,412**	**-2,422**	**-2,677**	**-2,633**	**-5,622**	**-17,894**

Source: CBO cost estimate of S. 954 as reported by the Senate Agriculture committee (http://cbo.gov/publication/44248, May 17, 2013),

Table 4. Score of Mandatory Programs in H.R. 1947 (House-Reported 2013 Farm Bill)

(change in annual outlays in millions of dollars, relative to baseline)

	Fiscal year										5- and 10-year totals	
	2014	2015	2016	2017	2018	2019	2020	2021	2022	2023	2014-18	2014-23
Title I - Commodity Programs												
Repeal Direct Payments	0	-4,095	-4,158	-4,538	-4,538	-4,538	-4,538	-4,538	-4,538	-4,538	-17,329	-40,019
Repeal Countercyclical Payments	0	0	-117	-182	-190	-215	-217	-207	-197	-194	-489	-1,519
Repeal Average Crop Revenue Election Payments	0	0	-1,336	-696	-462	-424	-413	-454	-429	-505	-2,494	-4,719
Farm Risk Management Election	0	0	3,368	3,467	3,244	2,733	2,603	2,698	2,563	2,693	10,079	23,369
Nonrecourse Marketing Assistance Loans	4	6	7	5	5	4	4	6	6	5	27	52
Sugar Program	0	0	0	0	0	0	0	0	0	0	0	0
Dairy Program	-35	10	23	11	35	77	97	53	82	83	44	436
Supplemental Agriculture Disaster Assistance	897	364	314	296	295	297	300	302	303	306	2,166	3,674
Administration	64	35	0	0	0	0	0	0	0	0	100	100
Subtotal, Title I	**931**	**-3,680**	**-1,899**	**-1,637**	**-1,611**	**-2,066**	**-2,164**	**-2,140**	**-2,210**	**-2,150**	**-7,896**	**-18,626**
Title II - Conservation												
Conservation Reserve Program	20	30	-191	-354	-396	-462	-451	-468	-502	-565	-891	-3,339
Conservation Stewardship Program	-11	-85	-147	-219	-290	-372	-446	-518	-591	-663	-752	-3,342
Environmental Quality Incentives Program	30	58	72	87	101	114	128	128	128	128	348	974
Agricultural Conservation Easement Program	28	149	252	285	191	83	40	27	16	16	905	1,087
Regional Conservation Partnership Program	-1	-3	-3	-3	-3	-3	-3	-3	-3	-3	-13	-28
Other Conservation Programs	47	100	85	48	17	4	4	4	4	4	297	317
Funding	10	10	10	10	10	10	10	10	10	10	50	100
Repeal of Wildlife Habitat Incentives Program	-17	-35	-44	-53	-61	-70	-79	-79	-79	-79	-210	-596
Subtotal, Title II	**106**	**224**	**34**	**-199**	**-431**	**-696**	**-797**	**-899**	**-1,017**	**-1,152**	**-266**	**-4,827**

	Fiscal year										5- and 10-year totals	
---	2014	2015	2016	2017	2018	2019	2020	2021	2022	2023	2014-18	2014-23
Title III - Trade	15	15	15	15	15	15	15	15	15	15	75	150
Title IV - Nutrition												
Retailers	-7	-8	-8	-8	-8	-8	-8	-8	-8	-8	-39	-79
Updating Program Eligibility	-535	-1,295	-1,295	-1,270	-1,240	-1,220	-1,200	-1,175	-1,165	-1,160	-5,635	-11,555
Standard Utility Allowances	-190	-840	-940	-950	-950	-950	-950	-960	-970	-990	-3,870	-8,690
Repeal Bonus Program	-48	-48	-48	-48	-48	-48	-48	-48	-48	-48	-240	-480
Pilot Projects to Reduce Dependency	3	5	10	10	2	0	0	0	0	0	30	30
Assistance for Community Food Projects	10	10	10	10	10	10	10	10	10	10	50	100
Emergency Food Assistance	20	20	21	21	21	22	22	23	23	24	103	217
Nutrition Education	-26	-25	-26	-26	-27	-28	-28	-29	-29	-30	-130	-274
Retailer Trafficking	5	5	5	5	5	5	5	5	5	5	25	50
Northern Mariana Islands Pilot Program	1	1	10	10	9	2	0	0	0	0	31	33
Interactions	5	15	15	15	15	15	15	15	15	15	65	140
Subtotal, Title IV	**-762**	**-2,160**	**-2,246**	**-2,231**	**-2,212**	**-2,200**	**-2,182**	**-2,167**	**-2,167**	**-2,182**	**-9,611**	**-20,509**
Title V - Credit	**0**	**0**	**0**	**0**	**0**	**0**	**0**	**0**	**0**	**0**	**0**	**0**
Title VI - Rural Development												
Rural Economic Development Loans and Grants	0	2	5	5	5	5	6	6	6	6	17	46
Value-Added Marketing Grants	0	18	15	15	2	0	0	0	0	0	50	50
Subtotal, Title VI	**0**	**20**	**20**	**20**	**7**	**5**	**6**	**6**	**6**	**6**	**67**	**96**
Title VII - Research, Extension, and Related Matters												
Organic Agriculture Research and Extension	10	16	20	20	20	10	4	0	0	0	86	100
Specialty Crop Research	26	40	53	54	60	63	65	65	65	65	232	555
Beginning Farmer and Rancher Development	5	10	16	20	20	15	10	4	0	0	71	100

	Fiscal year										5- and 10-year totals	
	2014	2015	2016	2017	2018	2019	2020	2021	2022	2023	2014-18	2014-23
Acceptance of Facility for Agricultural Research	0	1	1	1	1	1	0	0	0	0	4	5
Subtotal, Title VII	**41**	**67**	**90**	**95**	**101**	**89**	**79**	**69**	**65**	**65**	**394**	**760**
Title VIII - Forestry	**1**	**1**	**1**	**1**	**1**	**0**	**0**	**0**	**0**	**0**	**5**	**5**
Title IX - Energy	**0**	**0**	**0**	**0**	**0**	**0**	**0**	**0**	**0**	**0**	**0**	**0**
Title X - Horticulture												
Farmers Market and Local Food Promotion	30	30	30	30	30	0	0	0	0	0	150	150
Specialty Crop Block Grants	9	16	18	18	24	29	30	30	30	30	83	232
Plant Pest and Disease Management	3	8	9	10	16	20	22	24	25	25	46	161
Subtotal, Title X outlays	**42**	**53**	**57**	**58**	**69**	**49**	**52**	**54**	**55**	**55**	**279**	**543**
Revenue: Organic Product Promotion Orders	0	-2	-4	-4	-5	-5	-7	-7	-10	-10	-15	-54
Revenue: Christmas Tree Promotion Orders	0	0	-1	-1	-1	-1	-1	-1	-2	-2	-3	-10
Subtotal, Title X	**42**	**51**	**52**	**53**	**63**	**43**	**44**	**46**	**43**	**43**	**261**	**479**
Title XI - Crop Insurance												
Supplemental Coverage Option	26	254	335	366	433	454	484	484	502	511	1,414	3,850
Catasptrophic Crop Insurance Rerating	-4	-38	-50	-52	-52	-53	-54	-55	-55	-56	-196	-469
Enterprise Units Irrigated/Nonirrigated Crops	5	47	62	63	64	66	68	69	71	72	241	586
Adjustment in Average Producer History Yields	2	21	49	75	102	129	137	139	141	143	248	936
Equitable Relief for Specialty Crop Producers	127	36	37	5	0	0	0	0	0	0	205	205
Crop Production on Native Sod (Prairie Potholes)	0	-4	-8	-11	-15	-16	-16	-16	-16	-16	-38	-118
Coverage Level by Practice	0	2	17	20	21	21	21	22	22	22	60	168
Beginning Farmer and Rancher Provisions	2	20	26	28	31	34	35	36	36	36	106	283
Stacked Income Protection for Cotton	36	350	378	308	386	409	439	451	468	466	1,459	3,693
Peanut Revenue Crop Insurance	3	26	30	30	30	30	30	30	30	30	119	269

	Fiscal year										5- and 10-year totals	
	2014	2015	2016	2017	2018	2019	2020	2021	2022	2023	2014-18	2014-23
Implementation	2	21	16	15	15	14	2	0	0	0	69	85
Participation Effects of Commodity Programs	0	-9	-87	-104	-92	-63	-52	-60	-54	-53	-291	-574
Subtotal, Title XI	**199**	**725**	**805**	**744**	**923**	**1,024**	**1,093**	**1,101**	**1,145**	**1,155**	**3,396**	**8,914**
Title XII - Miscellaneous												
Outreach to Socially Disadvantaged Producers	5	8	10	10	10	5	2	0	0	0	43	50
Noninsured Crop Assistance Program	1	11	13	13	12	12	12	12	12	12	51	111
Subtotal, Title XII	**6**	**19**	**23**	**23**	**22**	**17**	**14**	**12**	**12**	**12**	**94**	**161**
Net Impact on the Deficit	**578**	**-4,717**	**-3,106**	**-3,117**	**-3,121**	**-3,769**	**-3,892**	**-3,958**	**-4,108**	**-4,188**	**-13,482**	**-33,397**

Source: CBO cost estimate of H.R. 1947 as reported by the House Agriculture committee (http://cbo.gov/publication/44271, May 23, 2013).

Farm Bill Budget and Baseline Issues

The budget situation is more difficult and uncertain this year than for recent farm bills because of the attention to the federal debt. Across-the-board reductions are occurring under an automatic budget sequestration process. The desire by many to redesign farm policy and reallocate or reduce the remaining farm bill baseline is driving much of the debate. Uncertainty persists about broader deficit reduction plans, some of which have targeted agricultural programs with mandatory funding. Much of that uncertainty affects the farm bill but is beyond the control of the agriculture committees. Moreover, some 2008 farm bill programs do not have a baseline to continue and will require budgetary offsets.

Thus, the political dynamics of sequestration and deficit reduction pose difficult questions about how much and when the farm bill baseline may be reduced. In an era of deficit reduction, Congress faces difficult choices about how much total support to provide for agriculture, and how to allocate it among competing constituencies.

Budget Sequestration

Sequestration is a process of automatic, largely across-the-board spending reductions under which budgetary resources are permanently canceled to enforce budget goals specified in statute. Many of the sequestration provisions currently used were authorized by the Balanced Budget and Emergency Deficit Control Act of 1985, as amended (Title II of P.L. 99-177, also known as the Gramm-Rudman-Hollings Act). The current sequestration requirements were included in the Budget Control Act of 2011 (BCA; P.L. 112-25) as a last resort to enforce deficit reduction.[20]

The nutrition programs and the Conservation Reserve Program in the farm bill are exempt from sequestration.[21] Other programs, including prior legal obligations in crop insurance and some of the farm commodity programs,[22] may be exempt, as determined by the Office of Management and Budget (OMB).

FY2013 Sequestration

Given the failure of the Joint Select Committee on Deficit Reduction to propose budget reductions by January 2012, and in the absence of a "grand bargain" for deficit reduction by Congress during the remainder of 2012,[23] budget sequestration was ordered on March 1, 2013.[24] Sequestration is reducing both discretionary budget authority and mandatory budget authority in FY2013 by $85 billion across the government. The sequestration rate is a reduction of 5.0% from

---

[20] CRS Report R42050, *Budget "Sequestration" and Selected Program Exemptions and Special Rules.*

[21] 2 U.S.C. 905 (g)(1)(A).

[22] 2 U.S.C. 906 (j).

[23] See CRS Report R41965, *The Budget Control Act of 2011* and CRS Report R42884, *The "Fiscal Cliff" and the American Taxpayer Relief Act of 2012.*

[24] White House, "Sequestration Order for Fiscal Year 2013," March 1, 2013, at http://www.whitehouse.gov/sites/default/files/2013sequestration-order-rel.pdf. The trigger and timing for sequestration was based on Section 302 of the BCA (P.L. 112-25) and a two-month extension in the American Taxpayer Relief Act of 2012 (P.L. 112-240).

non-defense discretionary spending and 5.1% from non-defense mandatory programs.[25] (These are lower rates of sequestration than were forecast previously, prior to some savings being achieved in the American Taxpayer Relief Act.)[26]

The OMB report on sequestration indicates that about $1.9 billion will be sequestered within FY2013 from accounts in Agriculture and related agencies appropriations—$1.2 billion from discretionary accounts and $700 million from mandatory accounts (**Table 5**). Nearly all of discretionary budget authority, about $23 billion, is subject to sequestration. About $14 billion of mandatory budget authority in Agriculture and related agencies programs is sequesterable, according to OMB. This latter amount is a fraction of total mandatory spending exceeding $100 million (including child nutrition), since most of SNAP and child nutrition are exempt from sequestration, and OMB has exempted most of crop insurance. The table shows that user-fee funded accounts and trust funds (including disaster payments) are subject to sequestration.

Table 5 presents sequestration amounts at the account or agency level, as outlined in the OMB report. But sequestration actually is implemented at the more detailed level of "programs, projects, and activities" (PPAs). PPAs are defined in different ways, but for accounts in appropriations acts, PPAs are delineated in the appropriation itself or in the accompanying appropriations committee reports. Other PPAs are delineated in the President's budget.[27]

Once the uniform sequestration rate is applied at the PPA level, executive branch agencies may take various actions to implement the reductions. These actions may include transferring funds between accounts (which is limited by statute and generally is not available to agencies without specific legislative or appropriations action), reprogramming funds within an account among one or more PPAs (usually subject to appropriations committee notification), managing procurement and contracting options, and furloughing agency personnel.[28]

To date, USDA has indicated how it intends to manage sequestration in two letters sent to Congress: one outlining furloughs and estimated effects prior to sequestration[29] and one in response to congressional questions after sequestration.[30]

Implementing sequestration at the PPA level may restrict the flexibility of the Administration to manage the reductions (e.g., requiring furloughs of employees, or canceling some desired activities while preserving portions of other activities). On the other hand, in the absence of new budget directions from Congress, sequestration at the PPA level preserves the intended allocation of resources that Congress more recently appropriated, albeit at a prorated basis.

---

[25] OMB, *Report to the Congress on the Joint Committee Sequestration for Fiscal Year 2013*, March 1, 2013, at http://www.whitehouse.gov/sites/default/files/omb/assets/legislative_reports/fy13ombjcsequestrationreport.pdf.

[26] OMB, *Report Pursuant to the Sequestration Transparency Act*, September 2012, at http://www.whitehouse.gov/sites/default/files/omb/assets/legislative_reports/stareport.pdf.

[27] 2 USC 902 (k)(2); Balanced Budget and Emergency Deficit Control Act, Section 256(k)(2), P.L. 99-177.

[28] CRS Report R42972, *Sequestration as a Budget Enforcement Process: Frequently Asked Questions*.

[29] USDA Secretary Vilsack, Letter on impacts of sequestration to Senate Appropriations Committee Chairwoman Mikulski, February 5, 2013, at http://www.appropriations.senate.gov/ht-full.cfm?method=hearings.download&id=cda06eef-0c7b-4d77-819e-d8fefb5f32db.

[30] USDA Secretary Vilsack, "Letter on impacts of sequestration to Senator Grassley," March 8, 2013, at http://www.grassley.senate.gov/about/upload/Signed-Copy-to-Sen-Grassley.pdf.

Table 5. Sequestration in FY2013 of Agriculture and Related Agencies Appropriations Accounts

(millions of dollars)

Account	Sequesterable Budget Authority	Sequestration rate: 5.0% discretionary 5.1% mandatory	Amount Sequestered in FY2013
Offices of Secretary and Chief Economist	27	5.0%	1
Office of Inspector General	86	5.0%	4
Buildings, facilities, and rental payments	232	5.0%	12
National Appeals Division	13	5.0%	1
Office of Civil Rights	21	5.0%	1
Hazardous materials management	4	5.0%	0
Department Administration	86	5.0%	4
Office of Communications	8	5.0%	0
General Counsel	40	5.0%	2
Agricultural Research Service	1,102	5.0%	55
National Institute of Food & Agriculture	1,213	5.0%	61
Economic Research Service	78	5.0%	4
National Agricultural Statistics Service	160	5.0%	8
Animal & Plant Health Inspection Service	825	5.0%	41
Other spending authority	18	5.0%	1
User fees (mandatory)	266	5.1%	14
Agricultural Marketing Service	84	5.0%	4
Section 32	792	5.1%	40
Other mandatory accounts	76	5.1%	4
Grain Inspection, Packers & Stockyards	38	5.0%	2
User fees (mandatory)	41	5.1%	2
Food Safety & Inspection Service	1,010	5.0%	51
User fees (discretionary)	45	5.0%	2
Farm Service Agency: Salaries and Expenses	1,254	5.0%	63
FSA Farm Loan Program	408	5.0%	20
Grassroots mediation; source water protection	8	5.0%	0
Risk Management Agency: Salaries & Expenses	75	5.0%	4
Federal Crop Insurance Corporation	58	5.1%	3
Commodity Credit Corporation	6,460	5.1%	329
Agricultural Disaster Relief Trust Fund	1,372	5.1%	70
Tobacco Trust Fund	960	5.1%	49
Conservation Operations	842	5.0%	42
Conservation mandatory programs	3,357	5.1%	171

Account	Sequesterable Budget Authority	Sequestration rate: 5.0% discretionary 5.1% mandatory	Amount Sequestered in FY2013
Watershed and Flood Prevention	180	5.0%	9
Watershed Rehabilitation Program	15	5.0%	1
Water Bank Program	8	5.0%	0
Rural Development Salaries and Expenses	183	5.0%	9
Rural Housing Service	1,529	5.0%	76
Rural Business-Cooperative Service	179	5.0%	9
Rural Energy for America Program (mandatory)	22	5.1%	1
Rural Utilities Service	591	5.0%	30
Nutrition Programs Administration	140	5.0%	7
WIC Program	6,659	5.0%	333
Child Nutrition Programs	49	5.1%	2
SNAP, Food & Nutrition Act Programs	93	5.1%	5
Commodity Assistance Programs	73	5.0%	4
Mandatory accounts	21	5.1%	1
Foreign Agric. Service: Salaries and Expenses	177	5.0%	9
Public Law (P.L.) 480	1,475	5.0%	74
McGovern-Dole Food for Education	185	5.0%	9
CCC Export Loan Salaries	3	5.0%	0
Food and Drug Administration	2,521	5.0%	126
User fees (discretionary)	1,328	5.0%	66
Other accounts (mandatory)	327	5.1%	17
Commodity Futures Trading Commission	206	5.0%	10
Mandatory accounts	13	5.1%	1
Subtotal of mandatory accounts	**13,907**	**5.1%**	**709**
Subtotal of discretionary accounts	**23,129**	**5.0%**	**1,156**
Total, Agriculture and Related Agencies Appropriations	**37,036**		**1,866**

Source: CRS, using *OMB Report to the Congress on the Joint Committee Sequestration for Fiscal Year 2013*, March 1, 2013, at http://www.whitehouse. gov/sites/default/files/omb/assets/legislative_reports/fy13ombjcsequestrationreport.pdf.

Sequestration in the FY2014-FY2023 Baseline

The May 2013 CBO baseline (**Table 1**), which was released after FY2013 sequestration was ordered by OMB as discussed above, includes a reduction over the FY2014-FY2023 period because of sequestration. This post-sequestration baseline is the scoring baseline that is used to evaluate the effects of the 2013 farm bill proposals. The May 2013 baseline for agricultural programs is $6.4 billion less over FY2014-FY2023 than it would have been without sequestration.[31] **Table 6** shows how the $6.4 billion reduction is allocated across years, titles, and programs in the farm bill proposals. These are the amounts that by which a hypothetically greater baseline (as if there were no sequestration) were reduced to reach the amounts in **Table 1**.

Table 6. Impact of Sequestration on the May 2013 CBO Baseline for FY2014-FY2023

(millions of dollars)

	Fiscal year					5- and 10-year totals	
	2014	2015	2016	2017	2018	2014-18	2014-23
Title I - Commodity Programs							
Direct Payments	-408	-408	-408	-408	-408	-2,040	-4,080
Title II - Conservation							
Conservation Stewardship Program	-84	-73	-73	-73	-73	-420	-750
Environmental Quality Incentives Program	-46	-65	-81	-95	-108	-412	-1,046
Wetlands Reserve Program	-19	-9	-2	0	0	-42	-42
Farm and Ranchland Protection Program	-5	-10	-12	-13	-15	-55	-130
Grassland Reserve Program	-1	-1	-1	0	0	-4	-4
Agricultural Water Enhancement Program	-3	-3	-4	-4	-4	-19	-39
Cheasapeake Bay Watershed Program	-2	-2	-3	-2	-3	-13	-28
Agricultural Management Assistance	-1	0	0	0	0	-1	-1
Wildlife Habitat Incentives Program	-2	-3	-3	-4	-6	-18	-48
Subtotal, Title II	**-163**	**-166**	**-179**	**-191**	**-209**	**-984**	**-2,088**
Title III - Trade							
Market Access Program	-10	-10	-10	-10	-10	-60	-110
Foreign Market Development Program	-2	-2	-2	-2	-2	-12	-22
Food for Progress Act	-2	-2	-2	-2	-2	-12	-22
Emerging Markets Program	-1	-1	-1	-1	-1	-6	-11
Technical Assistance for Specialty Crops	*	*	*	*	*	-2	-4
Subtotal, Title III	**-15**	**-15**	**-15**	**-15**	**-15**	**-92**	**-169**
Title X - Horticulture							
Specialty Crop Block Grants	-3	-3	-3	-3	-3	-16	-31
Total Changes in Direct Spending	**-589**	**-592**	**-605**	**-617**	**-635**	**-3,130**	**-6,364**

Source: CBO estimates of the 2013 farm bill drafts prior to markup for the Senate farm bill (http://cbo.gov/publication/44175, May 13, 2013) and the House bill (http://cbo.gov/publication/44177, May 13, 2013).

---

[31] The effect of sequestration on the baseline is explained in the initial CBO estimates of the farm bill drafts prior to markup for the Senate farm bill (p. 2 and Table 4, at http://cbo.gov/publication/44175, May 13, 2013) and the House bill (p. 2 and Table 4, at http://cbo.gov/publication/44177, May 13, 2013).

CBO noted in its initial scores of the Senate and House farm bill drafts before committee markup that, "if the current-law requirements concerning sequestration were repealed and the Congress subsequently enacted the committee's draft legislation, CBO estimates that it would reduce direct spending by $24.4 billion over the FY2014-2023 period."[32] The $24.4 billion reduction estimate is $6.4 billion more than the official score of the bill at that point in time, -$18.0 billion. Similar accounting applied to the House bill markup.

Statements by some that the farm bill proposals reduce spending by $24 billion (Senate) or $40 billion (House) are counting the existing sequestration savings as part of the reduction. It is true that CBO said that if there were no sequestration, the bills would save these amounts. However, in fact, the sequestration reductions already have occurred in the baseline without any farm bill action, and would remain in effect if no farm bill were enacted. Therefore, the reductions that would occur on the basis of enacting one of the farm bill proposals, relative to the May 2013 CBO baseline, are scored officially by CBO as $17.9 billion (Senate) and $33.4 billion (House).

Since hypothetically restoring the sequestration reduction to the baseline would increase the savings in the proposals by the same amount as the sequestration effect, the net spending of the bills—if they were adopted—is the same whether one quotes pre- or post-sequestration estimates ($955 billion for FY2014-FY2023 under the Senate bill; 940 billion under the House bill).

Nutrition Title Share of Farm Bill Baseline

The proportion and size of the farm bill budget contained in the nutrition title has increased over time. When the 2008 farm bill was enacted, the nutrition title was 67% of the 10-year total ($406 billion out of a $604 billion 10-year projected total).[33] Five years later, it is 79% of the total ($764 billion out of a $973 billion 10-year projected total). This trend does not mean, however, that the nutrition programs have grown at the expense of the agricultural programs.

In the CBO baseline, each program is evaluated separately to determine its own expected costs using the formulas in law. Baseline projections rise and fall based on changes in economic conditions. In recent years, the nutrition program baseline has risen because current and expected food assistance needs increased as an automatic safety net during the recession. At the same time, crop insurance baseline increased as expected crop market prices rose, causing the insured value of crops and premium subsidies to grow. Conversely, farm commodity program baseline fell as those market prices rose and less counter-cyclical price support is expected. The CBO baseline thus reflects expectations under current law. The allocation of baseline among titles and the size of each amount is not a zero-sum game when CBO updates the baseline projection over time.

Farm Bill Programs Without Baseline

The budget picture is further clouded by other factors. While some programs (like most farm commodity programs and nutrition assistance) have assumed future funding, other programs (mostly newer ones) do not. Thirty-seven programs that received mandatory funding throughout nearly all titles of the 2008 farm bill do not continue to have assured funding for the next farm bill. Continuing all of these programs could require an estimated $9 billion to $14 billion of

---

[32] Ibid, p. 2.

[33] See CRS Report R41195, *Actual Farm Bill Spending and Cost Estimates*.

offsets from other programs. If Congress desires to continue some of these programs, finding the offsets needed could be doubly difficult during a simultaneous baseline contraction from sequestration or deficit reduction. Also, new pay-as-you-go budget rules enacted in 2010 (P.L. 111-139) restrict some of the budget-related maneuvers that were used in past farm bills to offset new spending.[34]

The one-year extension of the 2008 farm bill in P.L. 112-240 did not provide any additional mandatory funding for any of the 37 programs without baseline.[35] In lieu of mandatory funding, the farm bill extension made numerous "authorizations of appropriations" to allow discretionary funding for FY2013, but this did not provide funding. Discretionary funding, subject to availability in a tight budget environment, conceptually could have been provided by the appropriations committees in a supplemental appropriation or the full-year FY2013 Agriculture appropriation in the year-long continuing resolution (P.L. 113-6).

Many of the programs may receive mandatory funding in the five-year farm bills being developed in the 113th Congress, though perhaps not for FY2013. The House and Senate Agriculture Committees envisioned providing funding for many of these programs in the five-year farm bills that were developed in 2012. For more information, see CRS Report R41433, *Expiring Farm Bill Programs Without a Budget Baseline*.

Possible Expiration and Reversion to Permanent Law

The farm commodity programs could become more expensive if outdated "permanent law" provisions are resurrected. A set of non-expiring provisions from the 1938 and 1949 farm bills, as amended, remain in statute, but have been suspended by the more recent farm bills. The current suspension of permanent law, as extended in P.L. 112-240, expires after the 2013 crop year (December 31, 2013, for dairy).

There are no official estimates of the budgetary effect of reverting to permanent law. But the support levels under permanent law are likely to be above even the currently high market prices for many commodities. This could result in greater subsidy outlays than under the current baseline. For more information, see CRS Report R42442, *Expiration and Extension of the 2008 Farm Bill*.

Government-Wide Deficit Reduction Proposals

In recent years, increasing attention has been given to reducing government spending and balancing the federal budget through comprehensive reforms. In February 2010, President Obama created the National Commission on Fiscal Responsibility and Reform, with bipartisan leaders, to identify changes to balance the budget. Since then, several other government-wide proposals have been made for deficit reduction, and most have included agriculture to some extent (**Table 7**).

---

[34] For example, timing shifts are no longer allowed to be counted as savings or revenue for statutory PAYGO (that is, shifting the timing of existing program payments by delaying an outlay beyond the budget window or accelerating a receipt into the budget window). P.L. 111-139, Section 4 (b)(1)(A); 2 U.S.C. 639 (a)(3)(C).

[35] CRS Report R42442, *Expiration and Extension of the 2008 Farm Bill*.

In these government-wide deficit reduction proposals, cuts from the agriculture committees' baseline range from $10 billion in the President's Fiscal Commission, $11 billion in the "Gang of Six" proposal, $30 billion in the Bipartisan Policy Center plan, $32 billion in the President's FY2013 budget, and $33 billion in House budget reconciliation instructions, to as much as $179 billion in the House-passed FY2013 budget resolution. These proposals often are compared to the $23 billion reduction offered by the leadership of the House and Senate Agriculture Committees in November 2011 to the Joint Select Committee of Deficit Reduction.

Each of these proposals specifically recommended some reduction to the farm commodity programs—often mentioning eliminating direct payments, but sometimes also with limits on farm payments or reductions to crop insurance. Export promotion programs and certain conservation programs also were commonly targeted. Only the House budget resolutions for FY2012 and FY2013, and to a much smaller extent the agriculture committees' bicameral recommendation to the Joint Select Committee on Deficit Reduction, recommend reductions to the nutrition program baseline. To date, none of these plans has been enacted. But together, they represent a range of common ideas and the visibility for deficit reduction of the agriculture and nutrition baselines.

Table 7. Broad Deficit Reduction Proposals That Affect Farm Bill Programs

Proposal	Total Farm Bill Reduction	Detailed Provisions	Individual Savings (-) or Costs (+)
1. Bipartisan Policy Center (Domenici-Rivlin Task Force, Nov. 2010)	$30 billion [2012-2020]	Reduce farm program spending by eliminating farm payments to producers with adjusted gross income greater than $250,000 and setting a lower maximum payment for direct payments.	-$15 billion
		Reduce subsidies to private crop insurance companies. Reduce premium subsidy for farmers from 60% to 50%.	-$9 billion
		Consolidate and cap certain agriculture conservation programs.	-$6 billion
2. President's Fiscal Commission (Simpson-Bowles, Dec. 2010)	$10 billion [2012-2020]	Reduce mandatory agricultural programs, including reductions in direct payments, limits on conservation programs (CSP and EQIP), and reductions for the Market Access Program.	-$15 billion
		Extend disaster assistance programs in the 2008 farm bill.	+$5 billion
3. House Budget Resolution for FY2012 (H.Con.Res. 34, Apr. 2011)	$178 billion [2012-2021]	Reduce direct payments, crop insurance subsidies, and export assistance programs.	-$30 billion
		Convert SNAP into an allotment tailored for each state.	-$127 billion
		Unspecified remainder, much of which is likely conservation.	-$21 billion
4. Gang of Six (July 2011)	$11 billion [10 years]	Require agriculture committees to reduce mandatory spending, and encourage them to protect SNAP (food stamps).	-$11 billion
5. President's Deficit Reduction Plan (Sept. 2011; amounts updated in Feb. 2012 for FY2013 budget request)	$32 billion [2013-2022]	Eliminate direct payments. (Ten-year baseline is $49 billion, but CBO assumes interaction effect from increased enrollment in ACRE. Net effect is shown.)	-$30 billion
		Reduce crop insurance outlays by (1) reducing administrative and overhead reimbursements to crop insurance companies and (2) reducing premium subsidies to farmers.	-$7.7 billion
		Extend disaster assistance programs in 2008 farm bill for five years, through 2017.	+$8 billion
		Reduce conservation payments by better targeting cost-effective programs. Reduce CRP by $1 billion and EQIP by $1 billion.	-$2 billion

Proposal	Total Farm Bill Reduction	Detailed Provisions	Individual Savings (-) or Costs (+)
6. House and Senate Agriculture Committees, for Joint Select Committee on Deficit Reduction (Oct. 2011)	$23 billion [10 years]	Specific proposal not released, but a draft indicates a plan could eliminate direct payments, develop a new farm safety net with crop insurance, and make changes to conservation, nutrition, and other farm bill programs. Reported savings included:	
		Farm commodity programs (net)	-$13 billion
		Conservation programs	-$6 billion
		Nutrition programs	-$4 billion
7. House Budget Resolution for FY2013 (H.Con.Res. 112, Mar. 2012)	$179 billion [2013-2022]	Budget resolution (recommendations):	
		Reduce direct payments, crop insurance subsidies, and export assistance programs.	-$29 billion
		Convert SNAP into an allotment tailored for each state.	-$134 billion
		Unspecified remainder, likely in conservation programs	-$16 billion
	$33.2 billion [2013-2022]	Reconciliation instructions, by April 27, 2012:	
		By April 27, 2012, the Agriculture committee must recommend to the Budget committee specific cuts for a $33.2 billion reduction over FY2012-2022; $8.2 billion over FY2012-2013; and $19.7 billion over FY2012-2017.	-$33.2 billion

Sources: CRS, compiled from the following documents:

(1) Bipartisan Policy Center, "Restoring America's Future," Nov. 2010, pp. 106-110, at http://www.bipartisan policy.org/sites/default/files/BPC%20FINAL%20REPORT%20FOR%20PRINTER%2002%2028%2011.pdf;

(2) National Commission on Fiscal Responsibility and Reform, "The Moment of Truth," Dec. 2010, p. 45, at http://www.fiscalcommission.gov/sites/fiscalcommission.gov/files/documents/TheMomentofTruth12_1_2010.pdf;

(3) H.Rept. 112-58 (for H.Con.Res. 34, the FY2012 Budget Resolution), Apr. 2011, pp. 76, 108, and 152;

(4) Gang of Six, "A Bipartisan Plan to Reduce Our Nation's Deficits," July 2011, p. 3, at http://warner.senate.gov/ public//index.cfm?p=gang-of-six http://assets.nationaljournal.com/pdf/071911ConradBudgetExecutiveSummary.pdf;

(5) The White House, "Living Within Our Means and Investing in the Future: The President's Plan for Economic Growth and Deficit Reduction," Sept. 2011, available at http://www.whitehouse.gov/sites/default/files/omb/ budget/fy2012/assets/jointcommitteereport.pdf; and USDA FY2013 Budget Summary, Feb. 2012, pp. 124-126, at http://www.obpa.usda.gov/budsum/FY13budsum.pdf;

(6) House and Senate Agriculture Committees, letter to Joint Select Committee on Deficit Reduction, Oct. 2011, at http://agriculture.house.gov/pdf/letters/jointletter111017.pdf; and press coverage of draft at http://www. iatp.org/files/Ag%20Committees%20Bicameral%20Agreement%20Draft%202011%20Super%20Committee.pdf; and Hagstrom Report, "Conrad: Farm Bill Content Now Moving Target," Nov. 8, 2011, at http://www.hagstrom report.com/news_files/110811_farmbill.html;

(7) H.Rept. 112-421(for H.Con.Res. 112, the FY2013 Budget Resolution), Mar. 2012, pp. 67-68, 100, 135, 159; and House Committee on Agriculture (minority), "FY2013 Budget-Implications for Agriculture," March 28, 2012, at http://democrats.agriculture.house.gov/inside/Pubs/ FY2013%20Republican%20Budget%20Implications%20for%20Agriculture.pdf.

Appendix. Scores of the 2012 Farm Bill Proposals

In the 112th Congress, both the House and Senate Agriculture Committees marked up drafts for a 2012 farm bill. The Senate passed its version (S. 3240) on June 21, 2012, by a vote of 64-35. The House Committee on Agriculture reported its version (H.R. 6083) on July 11, 2012, by a vote of 35-11. House floor action, however, never occurred, and a one-year extension was enacted (P.L. 112-240).

The Senate-passed and the House-reported bills in 2012 were scored twice, once in July 2012 (against the March 2012 baseline), and again in March 2013 (against the February 2013 baseline). Because the updated scores changed substantially as explained below, and because the amount of budgetary savings in those bills have been referenced in the 2013 debate, the scores of the 2012 farm bill proposals are worth noting.

In July 2012, the CBO scores of the 2012 bills indicated that the Senate-passed bill would have reduced the baseline by $23.1 billion over 10 years, a reduction of 2.3% from the March 2012 10-year baseline of $993 billion.[36] The House-reported bill would have reduced spending by $35.1 billion over 10 years, a reduction of 3.5%.[37] These are the savings that would have been achieved, against the March 2012 baseline, had the bills been enacted in 2012 during the 112th Congress (**Figure A-1**).

- Under the Senate bill, six titles would have received a combined $7.0 billion increase relative to their baselines, and four titles would have offer a combined budgetary reduction of $30.1 billion. The net reduction was $23.1 billion.

- Under the House bill, six titles would receive a combined $10.7 billion increase relative to their baselines, and three titles would offer a combined budgetary reduction of $45.8 billion. The net reduction was $35.1 billion.

In March 2013, CBO released updated scores of the two 2012 farm bill proposals.[38] The updated scores indicated that the 2012 Senate-passed bill would have reduce the baseline by $13.1 billion over 10 years, a reduction of 1.3% from the February 2013 10-year baseline of $976 billion. The House-reported bill would have reduced spending by $26.6 billion over 10 years, a reduction of 2.7% from the February 2013 baseline. These are the savings that would be achieved, against the February 2013 baseline, if the bills were enacted in 2013 during the 113th Congress (**Figure A-2**).

- Under the Senate bill, seven titles would have received a combined $7.8 billion increase relative to their baselines, and three titles would have offer a combined budgetary reduction of $20.9 billion. The net reduction was $13.1 billion.

- Under the House bill, seven titles would receive a combined $12.1 billion increase relative to their baselines, and three titles would offer a combined budgetary reduction of $38.7 billion. The net reduction was $26.6 billion.

---

[36] CBO, "Cost Estimate of S. 3240, Agriculture Reform, Food, and Jobs Act of 2012," July 6, 2012, at http://cbo.gov/publication/43417.

[37] CBO, "Cost Estimate of H.R. 6083, Federal Agriculture Reform and Risk Management Act of 2012," July 26, 2012, at http://cbo.gov/publication/43486.

[38] CBO, "Updated cost estimates of the farm bills that were considered in the Senate and the House during the 112th Congress," March 1, 2013, at http://cbo.gov/publication/43966.

Figure A-1. Original CBO Scores Farm Bill Proposals in 2012

(change in outlays over FY2013-FY2022, by farm bill title, relative to March 2012 CBO baseline)

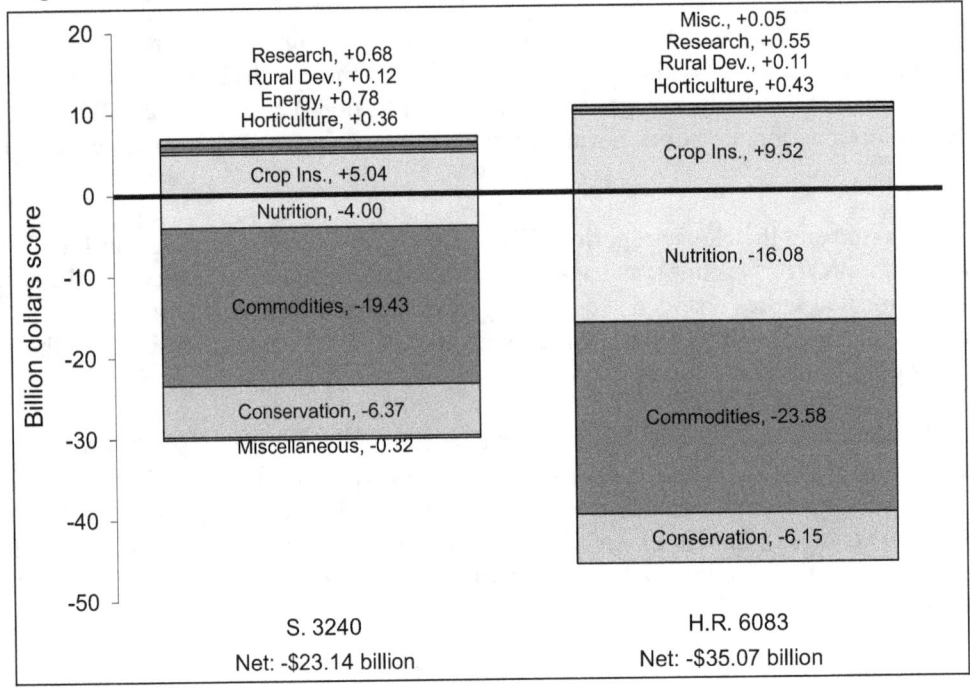

Source: CRS, using CBO cost estimate of S. 3240 (July 6, 2012, at http://cbo.gov/publication/43417) and H.R. 6083 (July 26, 2012, at http://cbo.gov/publication/43486).

Figure A-2. Updated CBO Scores Farm Bill Proposals in 2012

(change in outlays over FY2014-FY2023, by farm bill title, relative to February 2013 baseline)

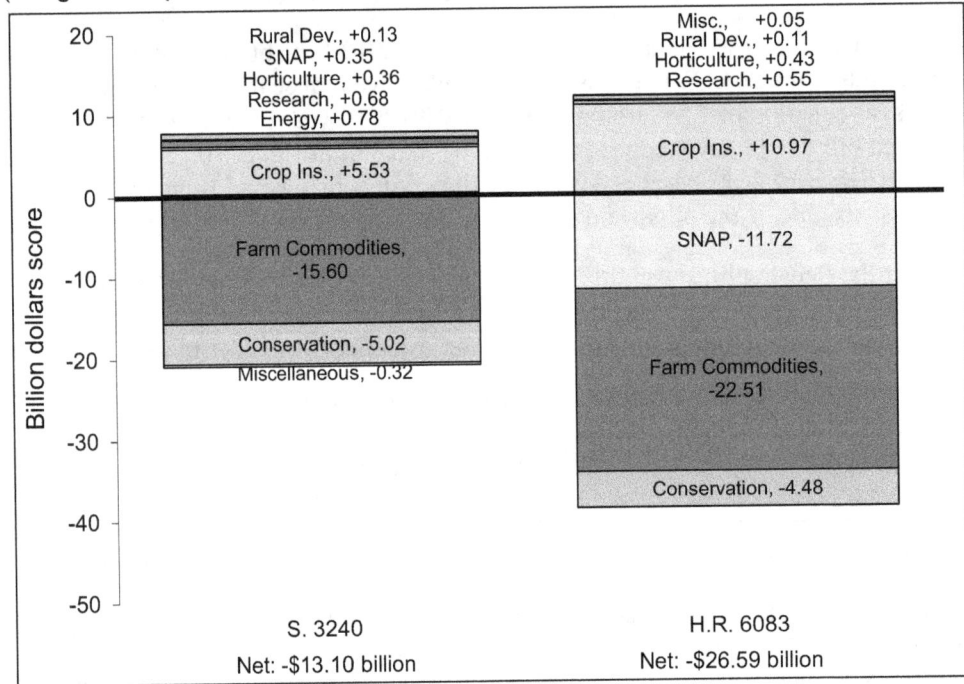

Source: CRS, using updated CBO cost estimate of S. 3240 and H.R. 6083 (March 1, 2013, at http://cbo.gov/sites/default/files/cbofiles/attachments/s3240_hr6083_Stabenow_Ltr.pdf).

Table A-1. Baseline and Scores of 2012 Farm Bill Proposals, by Title

(outlays in millions of dollars, 10-year totals)

2012 Farm Bill Titles	Original CBO Score (July 2012)			Updated CBO Score (March 2013)		
	10-year Baseline March 2012	CBO Score of Bill (change to baseline)		10-year Baseline February 2013	CBO Score of Bill (change to baseline)	
		S. 3240	H.R. 6083		S. 3240	H.R. 6083
I Farm Commodities	62,944	-19,428	-23,584	64,284	-15,596	-22,507
II Conservation	64,067	-6,374	-6,148	63,954	-5,021	-4,480
III Trade	3,442	+0	+0	3,435	+0	+0
IV Nutrition	772,109	-4,000	-16,075	760,542	+354	-11,715
V Credit	-2,665	+0	+0	-1,850	+0	+0
VI Rural Development	25	+115	+105	13	+131	+112
VII Research	214	+681	+546	111	+681	+546
VIII Forestry	9	+9	+4	3	+10	+4
IX Energy	750	+780	+0	243	+780	+5
X Horticulture	1,080	+360	+435	1,061	+359	+428
XI Crop Insurance	90,867	+5,036	+9,523	84,576	+5,526	+10,971
XII Miscellaneous	0	-319	+50	0	-319	+50
Total	**992,842**	**-23,140**	**-35,144**	**976,372**	**-13,095**	**-26,586**

Source: CRS, using the March 2012 and May 2013 CBO baselines by title (unpublished); CBO cost estimates of S. 3240 (July 6, 2012, at http://cbo.gov/publication/43417) and H.R. 6083 (July 26, 2012, at http://cbo.gov/publication/43486); and updated CBO cost estimate of S. 3240 and H.R. 6083 (March 1, 2013, at http://cbo.gov/sites/default/files/cbofiles/attachments/s3240_hr6083_Stabenow_Ltr.pdf).

Notes: The baseline and scores in 2012 are for the period FY2013-FY2022; the baseline and scores in 2013 are for the period FY2014-FY2023,

Table A-1 contains the data from the figures in tabular form, and includes the baselines against which the scores were made.

A consequence of the re-estimates is that the updated Senate score in 2013 was $10 billion less in savings than was scored in 2012; the updated House score was $9 billion less in savings than scored in 2012. That is, the same bills in the 113th Congress would achieve less budgetary savings than was expected in 2012, thus implying that modeling a new farm bill on the 2012 bills would cost more (save less) than might have been expected, unless additional changes were made.[39]

The updated scores in 2013 were different from the 2012 scores in two important ways: (1) they were relative to the February 2013 baseline insofar as expectations of the economy and commodity prices, and (2) they reflected new CBO analysis of the effect of the bills' provisions.

---

[39] Craig Jagger, "Why do CBO cost estimates change?," March 7, 2013, at http://agchallenge2050.org/farm-and-food-policy/2013/03/why-do-cbo-cost-estimates-change.

Among the differences accounting for the $10 billion change in the Senate bill's score was:

- $4.5 billion of savings that were no longer achieved from the nutrition title's standard utility allowance provision, given new information about implementation of the program;

- $2.4 billion of additional costs for the new Agricultural Risk Coverage program in Title I due to higher prices;

- $1.5 billion of additional costs for disaster assistance due to the severity of the 2012 drought; and

- $1.4 billion of additional conservation program costs.

Among the differences accounting for the $9 billion change in the House bill's score was:

- The same $4.5 billion of savings that were no longer achieved from the standard utility allowance provision,

- $1.7 billion of additional conservation program costs,

- $1.5 billion of additional crop insurance costs because of interaction with a new commodity program, and

- $1.1 billion of additional costs for disaster assistance due to the severity of the 2012 drought.

Author Contact Information

Jim Monke
Specialist in Agricultural Policy
jmonke@crs.loc.gov, 7-9664

www.ingramcontent.com/pod-product-compliance
Lightning Source LLC
Chambersburg PA
CBHW081402170526
45166CB00010B/3175